Praise for *Teach Up!*

"Developing into a master teacher is one of ... inclusive manual with sensible instruction... ....n unquestionably inten-sify the student-teacher bond, which is the central theme in the book. As an educator for 38 years, I am recommending *Teach Up!* because we need every classroom to be a bea-con of what Venola advocates: students who feel cared for, challenged, and successful."

—Clark Mershon, executive director,
Missouri Association of Secondary School Principals

"Venola just gets it! She offers an insightful and practical perspective for educators who want to strengthen their instructional practices and do it in a way that seeks to understand students—through relationships. If you are wondering who this book is for, my friend, it is indeed for you and everyone else who is serious about truly educat-ing students."

—Nautrie Jones, managing director, Teach For America

"As beginning and experienced educators stand at the dawn of a new teaching era, *Teach Up!* provides a clear and compelling path of inclusive strategies, intentional best prac-tices, and transformative takeaways that engage and guide the critical and creative think-ing of 21st-century learners. Venola Mason's exemplary focus, real-classroom work, dedication, and love for all stakeholders of the teaching and learning business is most evident! Teach Up and you will embrace the whole learner from restorative circles to excel-ebrations!"

—Dr. Rebecca Dashiell-Mitchell, assistant professor,
Clark Atlanta University, Atlanta, Georgia;
former principal, Atlanta Public Schools

"Venola Mason has written a must-have resource for all educators! Venola does a fan-tastic job taking educators through the important elements that are needed to cultivate strong relationships with students and families in their schools and classrooms. Her book *Teach Up!* offers practical strategies and ideas from her Teach Up! Tips, personal examples throughout every chapter, and PAUSE and REACT tool. The lesson ideas and relationship-building activities that are featured in the book are practical and can be used immediately in any classroom. This book works to push educators to be better for their students. I love how the focus in this book is on building a strong relationship with students, families, and the community. This is a wonderful instructional resource for any educator to have in their teacher toolbox."

—Kristin Gainer, fifth grade teacher, Pennsylvania

"Educators from all walks of life are seeking, now more than ever, authentic approaches to cultivate culturally responsive learning communities. Mason constructs a new type of relationship-building structure that pinpoints struggles and solutions to foster growth for both teachers and students. Mason guides us to aim high at the intersection of empathy, vulnerability, and resilience—resulting in remarkable achievement for all learners."

—Dr. Tawana Grover, superintendent,
Grand Island Public Schools, Grand Island, Nebraska

"The key to learning is relationships. Venola Mason provides readers with an important blueprint for how to build authentic relationships, as well as provide instructional rigor and cultural relevance for all students. Essential reading for every educator, this book is practical, insightful, and offers powerful anecdotes that will help educators Teach Up!"

—Tyrone Howard, professor of education; director, UCLA Pritzker Center for Strengthening Children and Families; director, Center for the Transformation of Schools; director, UCLA Black Male Institute; author, *Why Race and Culture Matter in Schools* and *All Students Must Thrive*

"For the past several years many in the US education system have called for our schools to move to rigor, relevance, and relationships as a way to organize their instructional programs. The nation's most rapidly improving schools have learned that the priority needs to be first on relationships then to relevance then to rigor. In *Teach Up!* Venola Mason has captured these school success stories in a way that can serve as a blueprint for all educators committed to improving student performance. A great book and a must-read!!"

—Willard Daggett, EdD, founding partner of the International Center for Leadership in Education (ICLE), author of *The Evolution of Education* and *Making Schools Work*

"Dear fellow educators,

"My name is Medard Thomas, and I am the proud principal of Columbus Magnet School, an arts-integrated school located in the heart of Norwalk, Connecticut. A few years ago, I had the extreme privilege of meeting Venola. She was brought into the district to coach school leaders on how to create and sustain a culture of high expectations and excellence in an educational setting. Additionally, Venola reinforced the power of creating strong partnerships among teachers, parents, and students because such strong relationships supported an environment of excellence.

"We embarked on a journey guided by ICLE's Collaborative Instructional Review rubrics. The rubrics were created in a way to clearly show the differences from basic to exceptional practices in the areas of rigor, relevance, and learner engagement. Venola took us on learning walks hosted by our schools to calibrate our understanding and discuss what we saw based upon the evidence we collected. We engaged in robust discussions, again, guided by the easy-to-read, yet powerful rubrics.

"Venola is a master teacher of teachers. Her philosophy and essence are grounded in providing the tools to draw out the best in educators. Her teaching style is rooted in trust. She is inspirational and gets you to believe in your power to lead with your head and your heart."

—Medard Thomas, principal, Columbus Magnet School K–8, Norwalk, Connecticut

Teach Up!

Empowering Educators Through Relationships, Rigor, and Relevance

Venola L. Mason

International Center for Leadership in Education.

International Center for Leadership in Education, Inc.
1587 Route 146
Rexford, New York 12148
www.LeaderEd.com
info@LeaderEd.com

ISBN: 978-0-358-56838-4

Printed in the United States of America.

1 2 3 4 5 6 7 8 9 10 0304 30 29 28 27 26 25 24 23 22 21

4500826495 ABCD

Contents

I write in dedication to you, my precious Jeffrey. To show you, son, that all things are possible when you have faith and work hard. Make your mama proud. I love you!

And to my mother, Paula Mason. This would not be possible without you. You taught me how to love, care for others, and survive. I hope I have made you proud. I love you, too!

Acknowledgments

I t takes a village to raise a child, and it also takes one to write a book. *Teach Up!* came to fruition through the love and support of many to whom I am truly grateful.

To my development team: Kate Gagnon, Jeff Leeson, and Karen Propp, words cannot express my gratitude for how you helped to bring my ideas and concepts to life in print. Our video conferences quickly became the highlight of my week, and your insights, expertise, and creativity were invaluable. You are my essence!

To my review team: Dr. Lisa Corbin, Lisa Wills, Nautrie Jones, and Matthew Thouin, thank you for understanding my vision and adding clarity, expression, and thoughtfulness so that it would come across to readers. You are my pulse!

To my colleagues at ICLE and HMH: thank you for all that you do in support of school districts across the country and to ensure that educators have the skills, resources, and tools necessary to serve children and families in a meaningful way. I have learned, and continue to learn, so much from you on a daily basis. I'm honored to work with such a great group of individuals who put children first. A special thanks to Dr. Bill Daggett for his visionary leadership in creating the foundation for this work 30 years ago. You are my heartbeat!

To my family and friends, thank you for your endless support. You are there when I need an ear to listen or a shoulder to lean on. I am eternally grateful to have such a strong network and know exactly where to go when I need to recharge. You are my breath!

To all educators across the world, thank you for the work you do on a daily basis to help students blossom. Most of your work goes unseen, but it is not unnoticed. Never give away your power or forget your strength. You are my soul!

About the Author

Venola L. Mason is driven by the belief that every student deserves a high-quality education that provides them many opportunities to lead and contribute in the world as they transition into adulthood. She is passionate about working with school-based and district-level educators to develop practicable solutions to increase student achievement and overall well-being.

Venola began her career in education as a Teach For America Metro Atlanta Corps member in 2003. She taught for five years in Atlanta Public Schools, closing the achievement gap by leading her students to consistently make one to three years of academic growth across all content areas. She also served as a site manager for The New Teacher Project (TNTP), where she managed the Atlanta Content Seminar program, a professional development program for K–12 teachers. During her last year with TNTP, she served as a central site manager to support the state approval process and launch of the Georgia Teaching Fellows program, an alternative teacher certification program.

In 2011, Venola served as the director of alternative certification for Teach For America Metro Atlanta. In this role she created the Teacher Leadership Development Program, an alternative certification program for Teach For America corps members and secured the program's designation as an accredited teacher preparation program through the Georgia Professional Standards Commission. In that same year, she joined the International Center for Leadership in Education (ICLE) as a leadership and instructional coach and supported school districts across the country in the areas of leadership, rigor and relevance, blended learning, and rigorous curriculum design.

Currently, Venola serves as an associate partner with ICLE. In this role, she continues to support school districts through her thought leadership and partnership. She strives to thoroughly understand their needs and offers professional solutions that will help them to meet their goals.

When Venola is not working, she loves spending time with family and friends, traveling (especially to the beach), and playing tennis.

About the International Center for Leadership in Education

The International Center for Leadership in Education (ICLE), a division of Houghton Mifflin Harcourt, challenges, inspires, and equips leaders and teachers to prepare their students for lifelong success. At the heart of all we do is the proven philosophy that the entire system must be aligned around instructional excellence—rooted in rigor, relevance, and relationships—to ensure every student is prepared for a successful future.

Founded in 1991 by Dr. Bill Daggett, ICLE, through its team of thought leaders and consultants, partners with schools and districts to implement innovative practices to scale through professional learning opportunities guided by the cornerstones of our work: the Daggett System for Effective Instruction® and the Rigor/Relevance Framework®. Additionally, ICLE shares successful practices that have a positive impact on student learning through keynote presentations, the Model Schools Conference, and a rich collection of publications. Learn more at LeaderEd.com.

Introduction

Take a moment to think back to when you were a K–12 student. Did you ever have a teacher who was passionate, engaging, and truly seemed to care about you? One who supported you and challenged you; who helped you grow and fulfill your potential? Maybe it was in grade school, middle school, or high school. It doesn't matter. If you were lucky enough to have this type of teacher, you can probably still name her or him regardless of how many years have passed.

I had this type of teacher. Her name was Ms. Toni Little. Ms. Little was my English teacher at Crenshaw High School in Los Angeles, California. She was, by any standard, a master teacher. She was so passionate about her content that it was contagious. Never before had I been so interested in literature and how the themes in some of these classic books were still relevant both in society and in my own life. She would have us fired up during classroom discussions. If you had been a fly on the wall, you would have never guessed we were discussing *The Great Gatsby* or *The Scarlet Letter*. She helped to bring these texts to life for us.

Beyond her passion for content, though, Ms. Little also made it a point to get to know all of her students. Our class felt like a family. If you were one of her students, you knew she cared about you. Personally, she would push my thinking through rigorous feedback, always asking me to make stronger connections and think more deeply about the character's motivations. I could talk to her about things going on in school, as well as in my personal life. She would listen patiently and give me helpful advice. She had very high expectations for me and could see a future for me that I couldn't quite picture for myself. She encouraged me to sign up for Advanced Placement classes and apply to colleges all across the country. She wanted me to broaden my horizons; to grow and flourish like the sprouting sunflower on the cover of this book.

I'll never forget Ms. Little.

When I decided to become a teacher, I wanted to have the same impact on my students as Ms. Little had on me. During my time in her class, a seed was planted deep within me which drove me to become an educator and fight for educational equity for all students, regardless of where they live or who their teacher is. From my experience, I came to believe that we as a society could do better in providing the opportunity and support students need to flourish.

Now pause to think about yourself as an educator. I have a feeling, since you're reading this book, that you would like to have this same impact on your students. You would like to design relevant and engaging lessons. You would like to help students develop, mature, and blossom.

Teach Up! is about fostering more profound, more meaningful learning by cultivating strong relationships that help students grow—and ultimately thrive. It's about how to move from being a good teacher to a great teacher; how to move from designing good lessons and precise assessment criteria to changing the lives of students. *Teach Up!* is about becoming the type of educator that students will remember decades later as the person who inspired them, challenged them, and elevated them.

The Power of Positive Teacher-Student Relationships

The idea of "teaching up" means to aim high by developing learning experiences that help all students reach new heights, even those students who may not see themselves capable of academic—and life—success. This includes a commitment to working with all students in a way that respects their individuality, motivates them as learners, and rewards their growth. Consequently, *Teach Up!* shows the power of positive teacher-student relationships and high academic expectations to increase educational equity. Building on the ICLE Relationships, Rigor, and Relevance model, the book provides educators with strategies proven to help *all* students excel at rigorous tasks while staying engaged in the classroom. This relationship-based approach encourages rigorous and relevant instruction that expands students' thinking, builds self-esteem and self-efficacy, and maximizes success.

In my experience as a classroom teacher and through the work I've done with organizations like The New Teacher Project, Teach For America, and currently the International Center for Leadership in Education, I have spent a lot of time in schools across the country. During this time, I have worked with teachers, instructional coaches, principals, district leaders, and superintendents to support their efforts in providing the best possible experiences for the students they serve. *Teach Up!* provides the strategies, techniques, and tools I have developed and used through these years of practice and consultation. Combined, these tools can help educators develop a dynamic practice that engages students and invigorates the classroom. In doing so, teachers can foster an optimistic, elevating approach to instructional design and implementation that helps *all* students reach their potential, regardless of their circumstances or grade level entry point.

During my time in education, I've met many good teachers—many well-intentioned people who work hard at designing lesson plans and grading assignments. But they're often frustrated. They feel that as well-intentioned as they are, they're not quite reaching their students. They're missing something, an almost magical ingredient that can tip them over into being that great, life-changing teacher. This ingredient is their ability to create the types of meaningful relationships that facilitate rigor and relevance in the classroom. When we're able to meet students where they are, we can help them grow. We can impart the hard-to-teach, hard-to-learn content to students who need extra support. As a result, we can witness growth in students not just academically, but also socially, emotionally, and behaviorally. In this way, think of relationships as the glue that connects students to rigor and relevance. We all know that if students have a person at school who cares about them, they'll show up to class ready to learn. It's that simple.

Designed for All Educators

Teach Up! is designed primarily for PK–12 educators, including teachers, instructional coaches, and building-level administrators. It is my sincere hope that teachers use this work to understand the impact that relationships, rigor, and relevance have on teaching and learning and feel more equipped to implement the research-based and practical ideas into their instruction. Instructional coaches and administrators will find this book useful for enhancing their own understanding of the topics discussed and for defining school-wide areas of focus for improving culture and student achievement. They can also use the content of the book as a guide for providing direct support to teachers through coaching conversations, professional learning communities (PLCs), and other developmental opportunities. The frameworks, tools, and ideas presented throughout *Teach Up!* will support the novice and the veteran alike in creating a rich, fruitful learning environment for students.

Clearly Explained, Readily Applied

Teach Up! provides guidance on how to create a culture for learning by building strong relationships with students. This includes showing how to engage students in rigorous tasks that help them to acquire skills and knowledge that will be meaningful to them outside of school. To help with classroom implementation, I provide concrete and practical strategies that can be implemented immediately into any school or classroom. To support these strategies, the book examines the importance of social and emotional learning (SEL), the impact of childhood trauma, and the influence of classroom environment. It then shifts to presenting evidence-based rubrics and step-by-step practices for building relationships and increasing the level of rigor and relevance in instructional tasks that may be implemented in any classroom, regardless of subject matter or grade level.

Chapter 1 of the book introduces the ICLE Relationships Framework and lays the foundation for building positive relationships with students by creating a classroom culture that is positive, welcoming, and inclusive. Chapter 2 outlines specific strategies to be used for building strong relationships with students through the lens of the ICLE Relationships Rubric. These are strategies that can be incorporated throughout the school year. Chapter 3 focuses on the impact of trauma on students' academic performance and behavior. In this chapter, readers will be introduced to my PAUSE and REACT tool, which provides guidance for how to leverage and strengthen relationships with *all* students. In Chapter 4, I define what rigor and relevance mean in the context of instruction. Readers will develop a deep understanding of the ICLE Rigor/Relevance Framework and learn how to use it to plan and assess instruction. In Chapter 5, I demonstrate how to plan with purpose to create tasks at varying levels of rigor and relevance by using the Rigor/Relevance Framework. This intentionality includes a backward design approach to ensure that instructional tasks are aligned with standards-based expectations. Next, Chapter 6 provides readers with guidance for maximizing rigor and relevance in instruction through "Quad D" learning, the highest level of the Rigor/Relevance Framework. At this level, students are engaged in instruction that allows them to apply the skills and concepts they have learned to solve real-world problems. Finally, Chapter 7 provides strategies for creating a school-wide culture that embodies the Teach Up! mindset and effectively leverages relationships, rigor, and relevance.

Research shows that, all circumstances being equal, teachers are the single most important factor in determining the amount of academic progress a student will make over the course of a year.[1] Summarizing the results of a comprehensive longitudinal study, Wright and his colleagues said, "The results of this study well document that the most important factor affecting student learning is the teacher. In addition, the results show wide variation in effectiveness among teachers. The immediate and clear implication of this finding is that seemingly more can be done to improve education by improving the effectiveness of teachers than by any other single factor."[2] This is why it is so critical that teachers are provided with the highest quality professional learning, coaching, and resources to help students reach their fullest potential. This book, quite simply, is about creating these experiences and achieving these results. *Teach Up!* introduces educators to practical ideas and strategies that can be implemented immediately to positively impact the climate and culture of schools and classrooms.

As you read through this book and begin implementing its strategies in your own classroom, remember that this is an iterative process. It takes time. It takes trial and error. And you'll likely make a few mistakes along the way. But teaching itself—especially great teaching—is a practice. It's not a destination or final goal; it's a continual process of designing, implementing, and reflecting. Jim Collins, in his best-selling book *Good to Great*, described the Flywheel Effect. In large organizations, the Flywheel Effect is the process of slowly building momentum until there's a sudden breakthrough that allows the wheel to turn faster and faster on its own.[3] In education it is similar. In building a great culture or strong teacher-student relationships, there is no single defining action, no one perfect decision, no miracle moment. Instead, the process is like pushing the heavy flywheel, slowly building momentum until the point of breakthrough. It's a continuum of positive interactions, small successes, and breakthroughs in which the sum of the parts is greater than the individual moments or solitary actions. And if a student experiences a string of these strong relationships, the impact becomes exponential.

Thinking about it this way may seem overwhelming. I get it. With constant pressure to develop and present engaging learning experiences and keep up with grading, it's hard not to wonder, "How can I do this? How can I get to know all of my students? How can I turn the flywheel? I'm just one person." But I firmly believe that teaching is one of the most important jobs—or callings—in the world. One teacher can change a child's life. Just like Ms. Little did for me. Just like another teacher likely did for you. And together, if we can change enough lives, we can change the world.

1

A Positive and **Welcoming** Culture for **Learning**

Take out a sticky note, sheet of paper, or open a note-taking app on your phone. Write down the name of a current student who could benefit from a better or stronger relationship with you. Take a few seconds to think about who that student really is. What are her interests? Whom does he live with? Is she confident? Does he have friends in class? You may have a difficult relationship with the student whose name you write down, or the relationship may just be OK, but choose a student who could benefit from an even better, stronger relationship with you. I ask you to do this exercise because I want you to have a specific student in mind when you think about who you're learning *for* in this chapter. At the end of this chapter, I'll ask you to look back at your note. By then you will have some concrete ideas and practical strategies that you can immediately use with that student.

My many firsthand experiences with students during my decades as a teacher and educator have helped me to understand the importance of positive teacher-student relationships and how closely they are related to academic success. I'm remembering a fourth-grade student named Clarissa. At the beginning of the school year, Clarissa was very quiet and withdrawn. She didn't interact much with me or with the other students in the class-room. Clarissa's grades suffered because her classroom participation was very low, and she didn't seem to put a lot of effort into completing her assignments. When I saw how little confidence she had in her daily life in the classroom—not enough to complete the necessary tasks—I made it a point to try to connect to her in every way I knew how.

The breakthrough came when I brought my dog, Sugar, to an after-school event. Clarissa immediately connected to Sugar; she patted her on the neck and seemed to just feel comfortable being around my little friendly dog. So I started talking to her about Sugar; telling her about all her funny habits and what she liked to eat. After that I used the topic of Sugar as a gateway to open a line of communication with Clarissa and to slowly build a relationship. In the morning, I made sure to spend an extra five minutes with Clarissa. I'd give her an update on whatever silly thing the dog had done. That made her happy and gave me an opening to ask questions to show that I cared about her well-being. How did she feel about the day ahead? How had the homework gone the night before? What did she think about this or that thing going on in the class? Slowly, she began to open up to me and to the rest of the class. Her confidence grew. She became more comfortable in the classroom environment.

By the end of that year, because of the relationship that I developed with Clarissa, she blossomed. She was actively engaged in classroom activities, interacting with her peers, and performing well academically. See, it wasn't that Clarissa didn't have the ability to be successful in my classroom, but that the conditions initially were not ripe for her to do so. I had to change my approach in order to help her to reach her full potential.

Strong teacher-student relationships are important for every child. Strong relationships help the students to feel more comfortable in the classroom environment and serve as a foundation for learning. They help to build a sense of trust, self-worth, accomplishment, and confidence. The simple fact is that a strong relationship with a teacher can make all the difference in a child's life.

We now have evidence to prove the positive impact of forming meaningful relationships with students and helping students develop real social-emotional skills. We have also developed new practices that we can use to meet the needs of the students that we serve. In this chapter you will learn why strong, positive relationships are important to supporting the whole child, how they contribute to academic success, and their central importance to your teaching. You will also learn about the role that the classroom environment plays in setting up student expectations, and to that end I will provide practical suggestions for how to create a positive and welcoming classroom environment to support students' relationship forming that will enable them to learn in the classroom. But first let's look at the relationship framework—its components and its relationship to rigor and relevance in the classroom.

A Relationships Framework

At ICLE, our work has long been grounded in the Rigor/Relevance Framework, which will be further explained in Chapter 3, that helps prepare students for college and careers. One way we do this is by providing teachers with a way to evaluate their current instruction through a four-quadrant view (A–D, along axes of rigor and relevance) to determine if their lessons and assessments are reaching high levels of rigor and high levels of relevance. More recently, we have learned that we also must address the relationship needs of our students if we are to address the whole child. We believe that when we focus on relationships, *with* rigor and relevance, we create a supportive environment where all students are able to learn.

Figure 1.1 (also reproduced in Appendix 1) shows how we've added relationships to the Rigor/Relevance Framework to create a new model that we call the Relationships Framework. This framework better represents the true association between the three R's: relationships, relevance, and rigor. As you can see, emotional skills, social and interpersonal skills, and cognitive

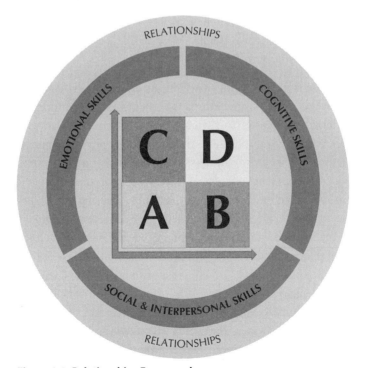

Figure 1.1 **Relationships Framework**

skills all build on one another. These three main relationship skills are interdependent; they make up the Relationships Framework.

Rigor has to do with the level of thinking or difficulty that's embedded in a task. A task is rigorous if it requires a student to think at high levels where they are synthesizing, evaluating, and creating. The level of task difficulty can differ from one student to another, but the rigor is embedded in the task and remains fixed. When we talk about relevance, it's not necessarily about lessons that connect to student's personal interests, hobbies, or pop culture, but about creating opportunities for students to use the skills they learn to solve realistic problems. Relationships are key to helping teachers create opportunities for students to use their skills and to develop the confidence to think harder and to strive for higher levels of difficulty. That's because relationships help build the skills—the emotional skills, the social and interpersonal skills, and the cognitive skills—that students need today, and will need in the future, in order to confront a rapidly changing world.

Relationships are also the foundation on which the three R's rest. The other two are not possible without first establishing strong relationships.

Relationships make relevance possible.
Relevance makes rigor possible.
Rigor makes life success possible.

The evidence is clear: building strong teacher-student relationships can ensure that our students are better adjusted, have more confidence, and perform better academically.[1] Social and emotional learning, now established as a bedrock in educating the whole child, comes largely through strong, positive relationships. Learning to develop the skills that make up positive relationships is of course important for its own sake in order to get along with others in and out of the classroom. What truly makes relationships so powerful and deserving of attention is that academic achievement and later success in adult life rests on our students' ability to continue to develop the strong relationships that facilitate social and emotional learning: becoming self-aware, regulating emotions, making responsible decisions, and empathizing with people from a range of cultural backgrounds. As educators we have the unique opportunity to positively impact the social well-being and academic success of students in ways that can foster a lasting influence in their lives well beyond their exit from our classrooms. Addressing students' relationship needs—in addition to their cognitive needs—is the proven way to do so.

Ideas for Increasing Student Cultural Awareness

TEACH UP! TIP

- **Get your students communicating.** Look for ways to connect your students with people who may be different from them. Help your class connect with other classes across the globe via online platforms like ePals.
- **Make it a celebration.** Consider hosting a virtual or in-person event that celebrates cultural diversity. You may tap into the community to host activities and perhaps prepare some dishes (or recipes) to share. Check out more ideas with a quick online search for "culture nights at school."
- **Enhance your curriculum.** There are many ready-to-use, free classroom lessons that support cultural awareness and global citizenship. One lesson bank that I highly recommend is the one curated by the thoughtful nonprofit, Teaching Tolerance. The resources span the grades and are searchable by themes like "race and ethnicity," "religion," and "immigration."

Relationships Are the "Why" of Teaching

Making the change to a classroom grounded in relationships, as well as rigor and relevance, isn't always easy. But the rewards—for our students and ourselves—are enormous. Some teachers will require support from leadership, time to make changes, and training. Primarily, however, the shift requires educators to understand and adopt a new vision of relationship-based learning as the "why" of teaching. Teachers who believe that nothing can be done if students are not prepared to learn or that students are to be blamed for struggling in the classroom must shift to a relationship framework that prioritizes students' emotional, social, and interpersonal learning. Developing the social, emotional, and interpersonal skills that make up strong, positive relationships is key to a teacher's own professional fulfillment as well to student success.

This new type of relationship-based learning includes the following changes:

- Students are actively engaged in learning that includes interpersonal and social growth as well as academic achievements.
- Failure and academic struggle are supported by relationship building.
- Positive reinforcement and relationship building replace blame and negative feedback.
- Classrooms thoughtfully and purposefully designed for a learning culture ensure that students are prepared to learn.

Many of you already follow these practices. As educators we have the opportunity—and responsibility—to build strong, positive relationships and interact closely with students to support their learning and make meaningful, lifelong differences in their lives.

When teachers confess that this new "why" of teaching sounds easier said than done or if they confide about feeling discouraged by difficult experiences with students, I tell them about a text I received from one of my former students. Years after she'd left my classroom, Marissa wrote to tell me that her aunt, who had raised her, had passed away. We'd lost contact with one another, and I was touched that Marissa chose to share the profoundly personal moment of losing a parent figure with me. Over the years, I have received similar texts and calls from former students to invite me to important events such as graduations, a celebration of a child's birth, or other special events in their lives. Some who have become teachers themselves write to share their excitement about *their* students. Again and again, when former students actively reach out to reconnect, it confirms to me that the relationships we forge are important and have a long-lasting impact on our lives—for teachers as well as students.

Relationships are central to why and how we teach. Relationships reward and touch us all in profound and lasting ways. Successful relationship building improves overall school variables: attendance, dropout rate, performance, extracurricular participation, behavior issues, and school culture. Those are the factors that ultimately determine student achievement and future life success as citizens of the world.

Now that you understand the "why" of building strong and positive relationships, let's begin to talk about the "how." There are many ways to encourage and support relationships in the classroom, but one of the first and arguably easiest steps is to create an inclusive culture in our classrooms and schools.

The Environmental Walk

Usually when I'm visiting schools, I do what I call an environmental walk before I go into classrooms. I like to look at what's on the walls and listen to what's coming down the hallways to get a feel for the culture and the climate of the school. A few years ago, when I did my environmental walk in a school building in Indiana, I knew exactly what type of day it was going to be: disheartening. The hallways were bare. There was no student work posted on the walls, no positive messages posted, and no evidence of goals or student accomplishments. As I walked down the hallways, I heard a lot of yelling and screaming and bickering coming from the classrooms.

Then I entered the classroom of the teacher whom I was coaching, whose name was Julie. All the students were sitting at their desks. They were quietly working on a reading comprehension worksheet from a story they had read the day before. Julie was busy behind her desk taking care of some administrative work. Her classroom was so quiet you could've heard the proverbial pin drop. I noticed a corner in the far back of the room. A little boy was sitting there alone. I gravitated toward this little boy because I was wondering: Why is he there all alone? Why isn't he engaged with the other students or the teacher?

Julie looked up from her desk and began to walk around the classroom, scanning students' work. But before she did that, the little boy raised his hand. He had his hand up for about 30 seconds, and then for about a minute. When he finally put his hand down he seemed a little frustrated because the teacher wasn't responding. He couldn't get her attention. His head fell, chin to chest, so I couldn't see his face. When Julie did her scan around the room, she noticed that the little boy's head was down. She walked over to his desk and looked at his paper, which was empty. And then she said, "David, how come you're not doing any of your work? What is the point of you coming to school every day if you're not even going to try? What's the use?"

What was it about this little boy that made him invisible to his teacher? What made her want to engage with him in that blaming way? If this is the kind of interaction that he's having in this classroom and with other adults in this building on a daily basis, what is the long-term impact? In such an environment, how is he going to make the strong, positive relationships that will allow him to learn? One thing we know is that if he's missing a lot of instructional time and he is struggling to do the work, then we can almost be sure that his reading is below grade level and that he is in danger of becoming another statistical dropout.

Julie had complete control of her classroom. Unlike many of the other classrooms in that particular school, her students were not making noise or looking at their phones. Although they seemed to be learning—most were busily filling out assigned worksheets—they were passive and quiet rather than actively engaged, which left little room for David to ask for help. Nor did it leave much room for the other students to help David or to learn from one another. Such classrooms are failing David and the many students like him. Classrooms formed around an environment that does not support relationship also do not hold joy or excitement for learning where each student feels they matter to their teacher and classmates.

In order to create the strong relationships needed to drive rigor and relevance—and support social and emotional learning—teachers must be intentional about creating a learning environment that is positive, welcoming, and inclusive. An inclusive classroom, where students feel they can be themselves and are actively seen, creates an environment where everyone's voice matters. In an inclusive environment that reflects students' cultures, all students feel cared for and challenged. The first steps you can make to improve the environmental walk and create a more inclusive classroom are practical and immediate.

Create an Engaging and Exciting Learning Space

Over the years of working as an educator and a professional educational consultant, I have often reflected on the importance of creating a quality learning environment. How does the physical environment of the classroom get students in the mood for learning?

A few years ago, I had the pleasure of working with a high school English teacher named Joseph. He was a first-year teacher and, unsurprisingly, full of energy and ideas. During one of our earlier coaching sessions, he explained that he was interested in incorporating a "station rotation model" in his classroom and needed some help understanding how he could successfully do so. When I observed his classroom, I noticed that he was trying to teach over his students. Subsequently, they were disengaged. It was upsetting for me to see Joseph trying so hard, and yet his students still weren't learning.

When we debriefed after the class, he shared that he was embarrassed by how poorly the lesson went. He even questioned whether or not he had made the right decision in becoming a teacher. He told me that if I observed the same group of students with their history teacher, I would think that it was a completely different bunch of kids. With their history teacher, he said, they participated and collaborated; they flat out learned.

Intrigued, I headed down the hall to visit the history teacher's classroom. And honestly, when I walked into her classroom even *my* attitude changed. The classroom was neat. It was organized and inviting. There were defined areas around the room for students to work, with easy access to all necessary materials and resources.

When the bell sounded, students walked in, put their belongings away neatly, and immediately got to work. With little direction, they knew exactly what to do. Throughout the class, the students worked excitedly. The teacher walked around the classroom and connected with various students individually. She asked some of them questions about their work, and with others, she checked in on personal issues.

When I met with Joseph again, we reflected on some of the differences between his class and the history teacher's class. In the end, we decided it was a difference in the classroom culture. The history teacher connected with all of her students. She was very purposeful about the design of her classroom to promote student learning. In essence, she had created a culture of learning that held students to high expectations and honored all student voices.

The key is this: our students pick up on how much care and pride we've put into setting up our classroom. And this, by extension, influences how they feel about coming to school every day.

That our environment is important to how we feel, operate, and even heal is well understood. Numerous studies have found that a calming environment, represented by natural-colored walls and access to window views of trees, helps relieve pain and anxiety in seriously ill children and adults.[2] This is also true for women giving birth and recovering surgery patients. Similarly, studies have shown that visually rich environments have a positive impact on student cognition.[3]

What impression do you aim to make on your students when they enter your classroom? The average student spends up to 1,260 hours in the classroom annually.[4] I've been in some classrooms where little attention was paid to how the space was set up or organized; as a consequence, the classroom culture suffered. What was obvious to me was even more obvious to the students: the teacher was not invested in the children's learning and had only spent the required amount of time setting up the room. If you are rushing to leave as soon as the bell rings, bag in hand, chances are that you don't want to be in the classroom any more than your students do!

Creating a space that you can be proud of and where students are excited to spend time over the 180 days of the school year is the first step in building relationships, establishing community, and genuine teaching. By being intentional about the way you set up your classroom, you can begin to create a positive culture that supports the strong, positive relationships that in turn encourage educational rigor and relevance.

Culture flourishes in spaces where you are very purposeful about your classroom design. It's so important to put careful thought into how students will move around the room throughout the day. You want to identify areas and arrange the furniture so that it's conducive to different types of learning: whole-group, small-group, and independent.

Purposeful and thoughtful rooms motivate students to want to be a part of an engaged community because it feels like a special space where people want to spend time. Setting up such a room will also help you to be very organized! You too will want to spend time in a carefully designed space!

Consider these practical, immediate tips to (re)design your classroom space to keep students engaged and excited in their learning environment. They are suggestions to help you begin to set up a space that is comfortable, inviting, and student-centered. See what works best for you and your classroom; as time goes on, you will want add your own tips. As you're creating this new, more inclusive space, ask yourself the following questions.

Is the Space Comfortable and Inviting?

When students walk into a classroom, they unconsciously make assumptions about the expectations of the teacher and the type of year they will have. If the walls are bare and the room is unorganized with little personality, the students may feel that the teacher doesn't care and is not invested in them. As a result, students may feel less valued and lower their own expectations for success. Instead, we want to create classroom spaces in

IDEAS FOR MAKING YOUR SPACE INVITING

In creating this type of space, consider the following tips:

- **Use color strategically.** A fresh coat of paint can breathe new life into a room. Research shows that color in classrooms can lead to higher productivity and student success. (Green is great for concentration, orange is a mood-lifter, and blue boosts productivity.)
- **Embrace flexible seating.** Varied seating options allow for student choice in deciding where they can work most comfortably and enjoyably. It also gives students more autonomy over choosing conditions that help them learn best.
- **Display inspirational quotes.** Strategically placed quotes in a classroom are a great way to create a welcoming tone and also reinforce positive messages.
- **Use the internet.** A simple search online will reveal many useful tips for designing the type of classroom that catalyzes participation, collaboration, and learning.

which students immediately feel welcomed, comfortable, and excited about learning.

You'll want to find a balance between how much color you add to the walls and the number of things you hang on the walls. If you hang a lot of bright colored student art and poster work you might want to stick to a more neutral background color for the walls. As in decorating any space, there's not one right way. Here's a chance to express your creativity and individual personality.

Is the Space Student-Centered?

Many times when designing classrooms we think about how we as adults will use the space. We consider where we will sit and work, how we will organize our materials, even where we will keep our personal belongings and snacks. Trust me, I know how essential snacks are! It's important, however, to shift our focus away from our needs and toward the students' needs.

IDEAS FOR A STUDENT-CENTERED CLASSROOM

- **Incorporate a theme.** This is a creative and fun way to unify the various spaces in the room. For example, a "Going Places" theme can use pictures and artifacts from around the world. Themes can change throughout the school year.
- **Create designated areas.** Ensure that all spaces are used purposefully so that students have the ability to work collaboratively, be creative, and display their work products.
- **Make materials accessible.** When students can easily access the materials they need, it fosters a sense of independence, and they take more ownership of completing assignments.

I had fun at the beginning of the school year helping a teacher redesign her classroom to be comfortable, inviting, and student-centered. We made a trip to the dollar store and purchased activity trays, storage bins, and picture frames. We searched school closets and found abandoned fabric and border that we used to create beautiful boards to display student work. These changes helped the students immediately feel excited about the learning space, a first step in forming positive classroom relationships.

How Will You Maintain Your Space?

With so many competing priorities, it can be difficult to maintain your classroom space throughout the school year. Luckily, all students regardless of their age can be a significant source of help in this area and free you up to focus on more pressing items. The internet, too, can help maintain your longer-term organization of materials.

Your classroom design speaks volumes about the learning experience in your space, even before you teach your very first lesson. With careful planning and a bit of creativity, you can create a space that will make students excited to learn. If you are unsure about what your design is communicating—or just seeking creative ideas—reach out to your students to get their opinions. Student input has other benefits, too. When students see

IDEAS FOR MAINTAINING YOUR CLASSROOM SPACE

- **Assign students jobs.** Delegate tasks to students so that at the end of each period, day, or during transitions, they can help to maintain the organization and tidiness of the classroom.
- **Use the cloud.** Store important documents and handouts in the cloud (Dropbox, iCloud, Google Drive, etc.). This will prevent unwanted piles of paperwork finding their home on your tables, floors, and in your cabinets.
- **Purge before breaks.** Refresh your classroom before major breaks (fall, winter, spring, and summer) by storing any resources or equipment that is no longer being used, updating anchor charts and student work displays, and discarding anything that doesn't have a place.

their ideas implemented they feel an increased sense of connectedness—and pride—in their classroom learning.

Getting Started

Chapter 2 will take up in detail strategies for building effective relationships, but the following are some of the basics to get you started at the beginning of the year—or tomorrow, if you need.

Be Personable with Your Students

As educators, it's necessary to set healthy boundaries between our personal lives and our students; however, it's also important for students to see us as human!

Try sharing information about yourself, your family, or even a pet to establish that human connection with your students. Students love to hear stories about your children or other important people in your life. They also like to know how you spend your time outside of school. My students knew that I loved playing tennis on the weekends—come Monday morning, they wanted to know if I "kicked some butt"!

Get to Know Your Students

It's important to cultivate your knowledge of your students on a personal level by learning what they do after school and how they spend their weekends. Your knowledge of their special interests or hobbies can be integrated into your instruction to make lessons more relatable. Find out whom your students live with and what responsibilities your students have at home. A clear view of students' family dynamics and lives outside of school provides a better understanding of their social interactions and the impact on their academic performance.

My former student Marissa, whom I mentioned earlier, was being cared for by an elderly aunt who was doing her best to provide for Marissa's basic needs. Knowing this, I checked in with Marissa in the mornings to see if she needed additional time or assistance with her homework. The more you know about students and their circumstances, the better you will be able to meet their individual needs.

Reach Out to Students in Need

Over the course of a year, students can face many challenges that negatively impact their ability to be at their best in school. Teachers have the responsibility of keeping an eye out for students who are struggling not only academically but also socially and emotionally—to lend them support through difficult times. Demonstrating to students that you care and are engaged in their overall well-being can make a big impact inside and outside the classroom.

Make Learning Fun!

Students learn best when learning is made fun! With so much pressure to stay on track with the pacing calendar, we sometimes forget to empathize with our students and create an enjoyable learning experience for them. Lessons should be relatable to students—designed to pique their interest and get them motivated to learn. Consider how to structure the tasks so that students are engaged and relish completing their assignments.

Your Sticky Note

Do you remember the student whose name you wrote down on the sticky note at the beginning of this chapter? Take a moment to think of that student again and write down three ways that you can strengthen your relationship. What can you do tomorrow? How can you set up your classroom to help that particular student feel cared for and appreciated as an individual? Be assured that however much stronger and more positive a relationship you can form you will be making that much more of a difference in that student's life and long-term success. What you do now truly matters!

To set up students for success, teachers must be intentional about creating a learning environment that helps them develop strong relationships with all students, especially those who are most in need. This culture should be positive. It should be welcoming and inclusive. Students should feel like they can be themselves, that they're being seen, that their culture is reflected, that their voice matters, that they will be challenged, and that they're cared for. They should be excited and experience joy when they walk into the classroom. This culture undergirds a strong, caring relationship between the teacher and the students—and, by extension, between the students.

This culture and the resulting relationships then lay the foundation for learning and prepare students socially and emotionally to have the confidence to tackle highly rigorous academic tasks. This may sound like a lot of extra work—I know how busy we all are as educators—but being intentional about relationships and culture actually makes our jobs easier, because it helps students to buy into the academic program, while simultaneously minimizing behavioral issues.

In Chapter 2, you will learn about three important concepts—connection, compassion, and vulnerability—that will inform specific strategies for building the relationships to support a classroom focused on rigor and relevance.

KEY TAKEAWAYS

- Relationships are central to why and how we teach. The relationships we forge are important and have long-lasting impacts on our lives.
- Supporting students' social and emotional wellness is a catalyst for building strong teacher-student relationships that can ensure they are better adjusted, have more confidence, and perform better academically.

- When we focus on rigor, relevance, *and* relationships, we create a supportive environment where all students are able to learn. Relationships are the foundation on which the three R's rest.
- The Relationships Framework is comprised of the emotional skills, the social and interpersonal skills, and the cognitive skills that students need today, and will need in the future, in order to confront a rapidly changing world.
- Designing purposeful, thoughtful classrooms where students immediately feel welcome, comfortable, and excited about learning builds positive culture.

2

Relationships

Strategies for Creating Connections

One day I received a call from a young fifth-grade teacher in Connecticut asking for my help. She was in tears as she described the difficulties she was having with her class. Students constantly challenged her lessons and were confrontational with one another. Fights were not uncommon. That week she'd had to put disruptive students into the hallway for time-outs until they calmed down and had sent three students to the principal's office. She felt stressed all the time and wasn't able to sleep at night. One thing she said particularly struck me: "I love kids and I believe in education, but I didn't expect teaching to be like this. I feel so angry and discouraged that many days I want to quit. Maybe I'm not tough or strict enough for my students."

Maybe you know a teacher who has had similar experiences or have felt discouraged yourself trying to maintain order with a difficult group of students. I certainly have. Although it may sound counterintuitive, research demonstrates that discipline and classroom control is not about becoming stricter. Instead, it's about becoming a more connected, compassionate, and vulnerable leader.

Over the next few months, as I worked with this particular teacher she learned to tap into these leadership qualities and to teach her students to relate to one another in positive ways that eventually transformed her classroom into an engaged learning environment. The concepts and relationship-building strategies I showed her are ones that you can use no matter how well-disciplined your classroom may be. Believe me when I say that building a learning environment where students feel safe and joyous, and where they are growing academically as well as emotionally, is not so much about keeping kids out of the principal's office as it is about understanding what makes for strong positive relationships and implementing the strategies to build such relationships.

In the first chapter I discussed the importance of strong relationships for students' happiness and development both in school and in their lives. Now that you understand the links that exist between emotional skills, interpersonal skills, and cognitive skills, let's learn some practical ways to develop those skills in students. In this chapter you will first learn about the three important indicators for building relationships—connection, compassion, and vulnerability—which are part of the ICLE Relationships Rubric. This is the "why" of the chapter. The second part of the chapter provides "Nine Relationship Strategies—Your Starter Kit" that supplies practical support for working with the Relationships Rubric. There are three relationship strategies for each of the three indicators, with specific suggestions for how you can implement each strategy into your classroom. This is the "how" of the chapter.

Some of the strategies in this chapter can be implemented immediately—many can be built into the everyday fabric of your learning environment—while other strategies can be saved for use on an as-needed basis. Learning the practical details about how to implement each of the relationship strategies will also give you more insight into how they create a classroom environment where students have positive relationships not only with you, but also with their peers. First, let's look at the ICLE Relationships Rubric, which has been helpful in my work with teachers and leaders and serves as a theoretical foundation for a classroom environment that's based on strong, positive relationships—exactly the types of relationships that build a culture to promote emotional, social, and cognitive learning.

TEACH UP! TIP

Build on a Solid Foundation

The start of the school year is the time to focus on connection. A trusting environment—creatively getting to know your students and helping them get to know each other—is best forged early. Encouraging your students to connect to others in the building will contribute to a strong school-wide community.

The Relationships Rubric

The Relationships Rubric is a framework for understanding, planning, and measuring a classroom based on strong, positive relationships. To build the rubric, those of us at ICLE reviewed available research, observed the strategies used in our nation's most rapidly improving schools, and relied on what we know about human connection and helping students feel seen, understood, valued, and cared for. Ultimately, we distilled the core components of building and nurturing relationships in the classroom down to three indicators: connection, compassion, and vulnerability. To see a table of the entire Relationships Rubric, as well as an overview and guide for using it, see Appendix 2. The complete rubric is also available for download at www .Leadered.com/TeachUp. Right now, let's define and discuss each indicator individually.

Connection Fosters Self-Awareness

We all need connection. When we connect with others there's a feeling of mutual openness, availability, and trust. Connecting with students not just on an academic level, but also on a personal level, is a prerequisite for relationship. The goal of connecting with students is to establish trust, the glue of relationships. Trust is necessary for students to feel psychologically safe enough to be themselves. Developing a trusting connection through relationship gives students the self-awareness to understand their strengths and weaknesses, to ask for help, to feel OK about themselves when they make the mistakes that accompany real learning, and to share struggles, either personal or academic, with their teacher. In a classroom that revolves around trusted connection and connected relationships:

- Students see their interests, passions, culture, personal lives, and family lives as relevant to learning and are given opportunities to incorporate them into learning tasks.
- The teacher offers scaffolded and personalized support to meet students where they are and address weaknesses.
- Students know their strengths, learn how to leverage them in learning, and feel supported in addressing weaknesses.
- The teacher creates an environment where students feel safe and shame-free when asking for help or making mistakes.

In a connected classroom, students also benefit deeply from connecting with one another and with their individual learning. Students who learn to connect to content and their learning process are marked for success. In short, connecting with and relating to people, to content, and to process creates engagement, an essential condition for learning.

Compassion Creates Social Awareness

Compassion literally means "to suffer together." It's the feeling that arises when you see another person's suffering and feel motivated to help relieve that suffering. Compassion involves empathy, which means you are feeling what another person is feeling, or sympathy, which means you understand what another person is feeling, but it is distinct from the other two in that it prompts you to take action. Compassion is at the root of many ethical and spiritual teachings and with good reason: when we extend compassion to others, we reject hurtful judgment, mitigate bias, and choose to lead with kindness. What's more, scientific research shows that when we feel compassion, our heart rate slows down, we bond better with others, and we feel the pleasure of helping others.

Teaching, known as one of the helping professions, demands compassion on many levels. Most of you already have a well-developed sense of compassion, but it's worthwhile to look more closely at the role compassion plays in building strong, positive relationships. Compassion is especially important and often particularly difficult when teachers are challenged by behavioral issues. Although it may sound counterintuitive, compassion can help us to better understand why a student is behaving poorly, which is a first step toward changing that behavior. The following conditions occur in a compassionate classroom.

- Instead of reflexively punishing a misbehaving student, the teacher tries to understand the root cause of the behavior. Instead of approaching the student actions by thinking "what is wrong with them," actions are approached from a "what happened to them" mindset. The goal is to avoid labeling the student negatively and help the student create a new, positive behavioral pattern.
- The teacher has a range of relationship-building strategies to help defuse tension and behavioral problems and help students reduce stress in real time.

- Students demonstrate self-compassion and compassion for their classmates.

This last point is important. When you model compassion and create opportunities for students to develop compassion, you create a compassionate classroom where understanding replaces blame and problem solving replaces punishment. When strong, positive relationships include compassion, students can begin to believe they are capable of overcoming others' biased perceptions, their own self-limiting beliefs, or entrenched detrimental behavior patterns.

Vulnerability Enables Courage That Leads to Self-Management

Think about the last time you tried something new. Perhaps you signed up for a new activity, or began a new job, or met a new person. You probably felt a bit shaky, nervous, or even scared. Vulnerability is that unstable feeling we get when we step out of our comfort zone or do something in which we might lose control or fail. I certainly feel vulnerable writing this book! What if I can't find the words to say what I mean? What if no one reads it? What if some readers don't like what I have to say? When I remind myself that writing a book, like any new challenge, naturally involves an ability to tolerate those fears and uncertainties, I can take a deep breath and summon up the where-withal to complete each chapter.

We tend not to value vulnerability, but it's a powerful indicator for success and relationships. Many people view vulnerability as a negative state or a synonym for weakness, but in fact psychologists recognize vulnerability as an important emotional pathway to openness and growth. In her research, University of Houston professor and best-selling author Brené Brown, links vulnerability to courage. She defines vulnerability as "uncertainty, risk, and emotional exposure."[1] In other words, it takes courage to allow ourselves to feel uncertain or to risk failure when we try something new. But a willingness to feel vulnerable—to experience the negative emotions that come with failure as well as the positive ones that come with success—is what allows us to grow, become resilient, and feel self-worth.

A classroom that's based on strong, positive relationships is one where everyone feels safe enough to be vulnerable. Students feel supported in tackling a difficult math problem or talking about a time when they felt sad because they understand that facing emotions is an act of courage rather than weakness. We can teach students to feel comfortable enough with uncertainty, frustration, failure, and confusion so that they grow emotionally and cognitively if we focus on the following.

- Teach students that learning is courageously vulnerable and presents typical highs (joy, satisfaction, curiosity) and lows (frustration, confusion, productive struggle).
- Reframe perceived setbacks and failures as normal and as opportunities to grow and develop resilience.
- Demonstrate vulnerability by sharing personal stories of setbacks and growth.

Equally important, we can approach learning with our students from what renowned psychologist and author Carol Dweck calls a "growth mindset" rather than a "fixed mindset."[2] Over 30 years ago, Carol Dweck studied the behavior of thousands of children and coined the terms *fixed mindset* and *growth mindset* to describe the underlying beliefs people have about learning and intelligence. Belief in a fixed mindset says that talent or intelligence is innate, that some people just *are* smart while others are not smart. Belief in a growth mindset means that people can get smarter if they make the effort to work harder. The feedback that teachers give is very important in fostering either a fixed or a growth mindset. For example, studies on different kinds of praise have shown that telling children they are smart encourages a fixed mindset, whereas praising hard work and effort cultivates a growth mindset. When students have a growth mindset, they take on challenges and learn from them, therefore increasing their abilities and achievement.

Acceptance, Trust, and Belonging

Remember that for many students, school is a primary place where relationships are established and nurtured. These relationships can be with classmates, teammates, administrators, support staff, or other adults in the school, but teachers are the primary point of daily contact for students. When kids feel that they are accepted for who they are, they're more likely to be accepting of others. Trust matters because it creates an increased confidence level, a sense of security, and the feeling for students that someone else cares about their well-being and success. Additionally, students who feel they have good relationships with both their teachers and peers experience a greater sense of belonging in school, which results in greater motivation to become engaged learners. All of these feelings—acceptance, trust, and belonging—are derived from care and safety when students believe teachers and peers see them as valuable; in turn, these students develop critical social and emotional skills that are further reinforced through caring relationships.

Nine Relationship Strategies—Your Starter Kit

Forming strong relationships takes practice, and the classroom environment is one where we can provide our students with plenty of practice. When we give our students opportunities to practice connection, which brings about self-awareness; compassion, which develops social awareness; and vulnerability, which enables courage and leads to growth and self-management, we are helping them develop crucial social-emotional skills that extend beyond the classroom today and into their future as global citizens. The next three sections offer nine relationship-building strategies—three for each indicator of the Relationships Rubric—that you can introduce and integrate into your classroom. For your convenience, I've included a summary of all nine strategies in Appendix 3. This summary is also available for download at www.Leadered.com/TeachUp. These strategies grow out of the coaching I have done over the years and have proven successful in creating trusting, engaged relationship-based classrooms. I am so happy to share them with you!

Relationship Strategies: Connection

Connection is something that you can build throughout the day, week, semester, and year. Try to make it a habit to look for opportunities throughout the day to share information about yourself with students as appropriate. You may want to share details about interests and hobbies or announcements about important life events in your family, such as weddings, births, and even deaths. Remember to ask students about themselves and their lives. How was your weekend? Do you have any pets? How many languages do people speak in your home? Exchanging personal information helps to build the trust and connection upon which relationships rest. Helping students to make authentic connections to content and to the classroom culture are also important for engaged learning.

In this section you will learn three strategies for building a more connected classroom. The "Joy Board" is a simple but effective strategy that allows each student to get to know one another via the happy feelings and events in their lives. "Classroom Meeting" can serve as a consistent and primary way to help students feel safe, seen, and valued in the classroom. "In the Know" is a way to use the process of getting to know your students to help them find meaningful connections to their learning. All three strategies reinforce one another and can be used concurrently in your classroom to build an interwoven, connected culture.

Joy Board

A simple way to help teachers and students get to know one another is to establish what I call a Joy Board.

Here's how it works. Have students reflect on something that has brought them joy in the last week or month. Instruct students to find an image or draw a picture to illustrate what they reflected on. Post the pictures on the Joy Board.

A Joy Board allows students to reflect on the positive things that happen in their lives and helps students find common interests or experiences. It also gives teachers information to incorporate into the class to improve or maintain culture.

Classroom Meeting

The classroom meetings that so many of you hold are integral to building the connections and relationships that make up classroom culture. They are a time for students to connect to one another and for you to connect to the class group. Below are some suggestions for morning meeting components. Feel free to include some or all, ignore what doesn't seem useful, and add your own. Classroom meetings can be used as a time for:

- Greetings and announcements
- Reviewing important cultural norms such as being respectful, setting or meeting goals, classroom cleanup, and paying attention
- Revisiting and reinforcing rules or commitments when needed

- Cooperative, community-building exercises or games
- Teachers and students to share whatever's top of mind and ask questions

Any and all of these activities can help students to get to know one another better. Meetings are also an opportunity for you to share something meaningful about yourself that you want students to know. Doing this helps to build connection, and it also models for students how to share their own meaningful information.

Classroom meetings are also a valuable time to check in and address any behavior or habits that negatively impact the culture. Having real discussions promotes cooperation and teamwork in a low-stakes environment, which helps students work better together in small groups. It also helps students to feel comfortable sharing their experiences and creates a safe environment that can carry over to the rest of the classroom.

In the Know

As teachers we can help students to find meaningful connections to specific lessons by tapping their life experiences and individual strengths. This can often happen as part of the process of students and teachers getting to know one another.

Here's a story about how this strategy works. A high schooler was at a loss for what topic to pursue when asked to create a solution to a problem that personally impacted her or her community. During the conference conversation, Laila's teacher asked questions about events in Laila's life. How many hours did she work at her after-school job? How was her sister? Did she have plans for the upcoming holiday? Laila shared that she wasn't looking forward to attending a family reunion because in the past such events were always "so boring" and catered only to the older family members. "You're so organized and such a good planner," said the teacher as a way to highlight genuine strengths she'd observed in her student. "Maybe you could use those talents to do something about the family reunion for the assignment." After a little more conversation, Laila decided to create a plan for the event that would make it enjoyable for all family members regardless of age. Having made that connection to the assignment, Laila got very excited about her project and became engaged in creating a solution that she could actually share with her family.

The more you and your students know about each other, the stronger and more authentic will be your relationships and the better students will engage in learning, feel more comfortable asking for help, and more readily share personal or academic struggles.

Relationship Strategies: Compassion

As educators, when we are compassionate we can see students as whole children. When students receive compassion from us and from their peers, they are better able to grasp rigorous and relevant concepts. Compassion means leading with empathy rather than judgment. Compassion helps us better understand the root cause of behavioral issues. Just as the culture of a relationship-based classroom builds students' awareness of each other as social beings, learning to interact positively with one another also requires compassion.

Creating a compassionate classroom means focusing more often on the positives about your students than the negatives. To that end, I encourage complimenting students as often as you can; this will help them become excited and engaged about school. Everyone knows about contacting parents with a note or phone call when a student has misbehaved. Why should contact between school and home be only negative? Sending notes home to parents, texting, or even calling them when a student has shone is another way to build the positive feelings that enter into strong relationships in a compassionate school culture.

In this section I will introduce you to three strategies for building a more compassionate classroom. "Yes, That's Me!" is a simple but effective strategy that allows each student to feel honored and celebrated for who they are. "Notice! Empathize! Act!" is a less concrete but powerful learning tool to help students develop compassion for one another. "Restorative Circles" is a way to restore balance and understanding in a classroom when a student has done something wrong or misbehaved in some way that affects others. In addition to their impact on your classroom, these strategies provide students with lifelong relationship skills that they can use to handle conflict and misunderstandings as citizens in the world.

Yes, That's Me!

The underlying concept in this strategy is that *every* student in the class is worthy of honor and celebration. Make sure to mix up whom you honor by choosing students who may be unpopular as well as popular and students who may be struggling academically as well as those who excel. Over the course of the semester or year ensure that every student has the opportunity to be recognized.

1. Choose a student to honor.
2. Direct the other students to write compliments on a sticky note about the chosen student.
3. Allow the honored student to read the notes aloud and allow the other students to add commentary.
4. Lead a Yes, That's Me! debrief with the class for the honored student to share with peers their feelings about their experience.

You might want to post a board or a large piece of paper that has the name and even a picture of the student who is being honored. Students can then attach their sticky notes to the board or write on it directly. You can guide students to write about acts of kindness they noticed about their classmate as well as specific talents or accomplishments. When you lead the debrief with the student you can ask, "How did it feel to be appreciated in this way? What did you learn about yourself? About your classmates?"

You'll notice that this strategy helps students to get in the habit of looking for positive things to say about each other. In the long-term, it helps to build compassionate rapport between your students and the classroom culture.

Notice! Empathize! Act!

How do we teach students to demonstrate support and empathy for their peers? How do we support peer relationships in and out of the classroom that engage student learning for rigor and relevance? One way is to teach the students the three part strategy I call Notice! Empathize! Act! Unlike some of the other relationship-building strategies that rely on consistency to build positive habits into the classroom culture, this one is implemented as needed. The first step is noticing others to determine when it's appropriate and needed.

Here's a story to illustrate how the strategy works. A middle school teacher named Therese noticed that her students were becoming cliquish, negatively impacting the classroom culture. Students were less eager to work collaboratively on projects and reluctant to speak up during classroom discussions. Therese decided to pose a general question to the class: Did they think cliques were helpful or harmful? A lively debate ensued, with students weighing in on both sides. Then, a new student opened up, saying that she was considering transferring back to her old school. When other students asked why, she explained that she felt isolated and didn't feel she fit in with any of the classroom groups. That discussion made a serious impact. Over the next couple of days, individual students came up to Therese to tell her how bad they felt that their classmate felt left out. Therese listened and encouraged the students to act in ways to make their classmate feel more included.

As this story illustrates, Notice! Empathize! Act! can require discretion and planning. Instead of directly confronting the cliquish middle schoolers with their behavior, Therese skillfully led the class to discuss cliques as a general topic, thereby opening the gate for the students to talk about their personal feelings, recognize their effects on others, and come up with actions to remedy the situation.

Restorative Circles

In a relationship-based classroom, Restorative Circles are used to replace punitive forms of discipline and to develop the compassion for social aware-ness. Rather than focusing on what the student has done wrong or what rules have been violated, Restorative Circles help identify who has been hurt and what must be done to repair the harm. Restorative Circles provide an opportunity for the class to come together as a group to address harmful behavior in a process that explores harms and needs, responsibilities, and consequence. Everyone must work together to develop an agreement or plan that resolves the issue. At the end of a Restorative Circles experience, everyone needs to feel satisfied about the process and the outcome.

When a student gets in trouble, instead of automatically punishing them, have the student fill out cards that you have prepared that have writing prompts such as:

"I did _____ because I _____."
"I feel _____."
"I wish that I had _____."

These cards can form the basis for Restorative Circles sessions. Make sure to also allow other students and you the teacher to share how the student's actions made them feel and how it impacted them. The class must attempt to come to a consensus or resolution as a group.

Restorative Circles allow a class to come together and decide on a course of action to address a problem. They allow each student to express their feelings and opinions. Restorative Circles are equally important in proactively building the relationships and skills students need to support one another and collectively address the challenges they face not only in your classroom, but in conflicts they will face in their future and out in the world.

Relationship Strategies: Vulnerability

After working for a couple of months with an elementary teacher in Michigan, I was in the classroom the morning he taught a reading comprehension lesson on cause and effect. James began the day's lesson by telling the students a story about when he played football in high school. He remembered one Friday night when the coach told the team to get plenty of rest because they had a big scrimmage game the following Saturday morning. But when James was invited by a friend, who was not on the team, to a party, he decided to go. As you can imagine, he didn't get to bed until very late, and during the scrimmage game the next morning did not perform well because he was tired and irritable. Because of his poor performance that Saturday, he did not qualify to play in the upcoming playoff game. He was devastated and his coach was disappointed. James emphasized to the class that if had listened to his coach he would have been one of the starters. He labeled as "cause" the fact that he went out partying on a Friday night and the "effect" as having performed poorly because he was tired and therefore was not eligible for the playoffs.

Several things are great about this story. First, it helps students understand the content (the mechanisms of cause and effect) by contextualizing it into a relatable event. Second, it allows students to learn more about their teacher—that he used to play football. If a student also shares that interest, the door is opened for another point of connection for the teacher and that particular student. Perhaps most importantly, the story shows that James is willing to share a vulnerable moment from his past. He made a mistake by not getting enough sleep on the Friday before the scrimmage game. He didn't handle the situation as well as he might have. When he told the students that he'd "learned his lesson" and became better at saying no to invitations that would result in less sleep and poor performance the next day, he demonstrated the self-management and growth that vulnerability engenders.

The classroom strategies to help students become more comfortable with vulnerability focus on three aspects of it as an indicator. "Check the Tank" allows students to share and receive peer support for emotions whether they feel happy, confused, or angry, helping to normalize all emotions. "Level Up" gives students an opportunity to reflect on situations and interactions where they wish the outcome had been different in order to make better decisions for the next time. "Stretch Out" is about setting high expectations and helping students think about what they would like to accomplish personally and academically during the school year, even if they experience setbacks along the way.

Check the Tank

This strategy gives students the opportunity to acknowledge and share their emotions. Through this practice students will get comfortable working through negative emotions in a productive way and will also have the opportunity to share good news or bright spots.

- Each student quickly shares their current mood using any of the following: emoji, song, #hashtag, etc.
- Two or three students are invited to share their response along with an explanation to the class.
- Students who are listening can ask a question, share a connection, or offer some advice.
- The teacher listens and follows up with students who are in need.

Some teachers provide students with a bank of emojis to draw upon (smiley face, teary face, heart, thumbs up), but you may also have students draw an emoji and hold it up for the class. Students can say, "Hashtag, I've been better," or "Hashtag, greatest day ever," or "Hashtag, I'm drowning." Share songs by their titles.

Students who are listening have the opportunity to empathize, connect, and offer up a positive resolution. The teacher can check in with students, even if they didn't share a response, to see how they are handling their emotions and if they need a listening ear.

Level Up

You could introduce this strategy at the beginning of the year, but it's also one that you can create today and start using tomorrow. The three-part exercise allows students to share experiences with one another where they felt vulnerable and recognize that ultimately they have control over how they respond in various situations.

1. A student shares with the class a personally challenging experience that did not have a positive outcome.
2. The class listens and responds with thoughts about how they might handle the situation.
3. The student shares how she handled the experience and how she would do things differently had she had advice from classmates.

For example, a student athlete could tell the class about being invited to a Friday night party when he knows he will have to get up early Saturday morning for a challenging game. Students could then offer suggestions such as, "Don't go to the party," or "Go to the party but come home early," or "You'll be fine. Go to the party." Then the student could share that he went to the party, did not come home early, was too tired for the Saturday morning game, and if offered the opportunity again, would choose to stay home instead of going to the party.

Level Up teaches students how to reflect on their own behavior in past experiences and collaborate on problem solving. It also gives us a concrete way to keep in touch with problems or challenges students may be facing and gives us an opportunity to respond.

Stretch Out

This strategy allows students to set ambitious goals for themselves and take the necessary actions to meet those goals. First, have students think about what they would like to accomplish personally and academically during the school year. Push them to set goals that seem difficult for them or that allow them to venture into something new. Students record their goals in journals, a terrific method for documenting their experiences and tracking their progress.

- Students record no more than four goals in a journal: two personal and two academic goals.

- In the journal, first students create a plan for how they will meet their goals. Remember to provide regular opportunities for students to document their process and setbacks.
- Teacher reads the student journals periodically and shares insights with the students about their entries.

Students can also conference together in small groups to share setbacks and progress to get input from their peers. As goals are achieved students can share with the class what their goal was and how they went about achieving that goal, including the setbacks and how they overcame them.

Relationship Strategies Build Classroom Order

Remember the distraught teacher who asked me for help that I mentioned at the beginning of this chapter? Together we reflected on the classroom she wanted to establish and identified strategies she could use to get there. She began holding morning meetings to connect with students. When we began working together she held many Restorative Circles in which students could talk about their problems with school and come up with workable solutions. Yes, That's Me! was always a bright spot. Although it sounds simple, another strategy that really helped to focus on relationship building was for the teacher to take the time to prepare lesson plans and materials thoroughly *before* coming to class so that she could spend extra moments throughout the day connecting with individual students. A turning point was when teacher and students created a class slogan they could use to support one another in achieving their academic goals.

Supportive social relationships are emotionally sustaining, meaning they enhance mental and physical health. One of the reasons supportive relationships work to restore calm and order to a classroom is because they provide a sense of what psychologists and sociologists call a sense of personal control, defined as the belief that we can control, or at least influence, our lives through personal decisions and actions. This is true of everyone but is even more important for our students who are still developing their own identities and finding their place in the world.

In the next chapter, you will learn about why strong teacher-student relationships can be especially powerful supports to our students who struggle academically and/or behaviorally and who may have suffered trauma or adverse childhood experiences. To that end I will provide more strategies—including my PAUSE and REACT tool—that you can use to leverage the positive relationships you have with students to support them when they are in need.

KEY TAKEAWAYS

- Connection, compassion, and vulnerability are the three main indicators in the Relationships Rubric.
- Developing a trusting connection by getting to know one another gives students the self-awareness to feel OK when they make mistakes, connect content to experiences outside the classroom, and tap into individual strengths to accelerate learning.
- Compassion, the feeling that arises when you see another person's suffering and feel motivated to help relieve that suffering, develops social-emotional awareness.
- Vulnerability, defined as uncertainty, risk, and emotional exposure, is a pathway to openness, growth, self-regulation, and academic success.
- Implementing relationship-building strategies that support connection, compassion, and vulnerability creates a classroom learning environment in which all students can thrive.

3

PAUSE and REACT

A Tool for Supporting All Students

One day, a new a student named Rose walked into my fourth-grade class-room. School had begun two months earlier, which meant that she was unfamiliar with the foundational work and culture I'd already established in the class. I greeted Rose in the same way I greet all my students. "Good morning, Suga. How are you?" Rose gave me a look that said: *What's good about the morning and why should I answer you?*

That week, I went out with my class during recess and stood on the sidelines, as I do with any new student to make sure she is fitting in with the group. I noticed that Rose was always alone and standing off to herself.

"Hey, Stephanie," I said to another student, one whom I knew to be especially friendly. "How come you're not playing with Rose?"

"Ms. Mason, Rose is mean. She doesn't like any of us."

"Rose is mean?" That surprised me because Rose seemed like such a quiet and shy girl. I resolved then that I would pay close attention to figure out what was going on with Rose. Why was she withdrawn? Why didn't she want to play with the other kids? Why did they perceive her as mean?

As it turned out, Rose had a secret, one that took time and attention to learn.

I sat down with Rose to talk with her and get to know her better. I asked her about her family and learned that she had six siblings at home, of varying ages, from a baby to a 19-year-old brother. I asked what she liked to do outside of school, and she told me about the TV shows she watched. I could see she was responding to my attention and genuine interest in who she was, and the walls she had put around herself began to come down. I was surprised when she told me she'd already attended five different schools and concerned when she told me her father had died when she was little, and that she didn't like her mother's new husband. Even though she'd opened up a little bit to me, in the week that followed she continued to hold herself apart from the other students and didn't seem to be making any friends. She wasn't completing any of the academic work, either.

As with all new students, I gave Rose a diagnostic test to determine in what level reading group she should be placed. When I administer diagnostics, I always begin one grade below the actual grade and then, depending on the results, I test one grade up or one grade down. Well, Rose did not pass the third grade reading test. She did not pass the second grade reading test. Not the first grade, either. In fact, she barely knew her letters or sounds. Rose's secret was that she could not read! She was mean to the other students because she didn't want anyone to find out her secret. She was ashamed, and afraid she'd be teased or bullied for not knowing how to read. That explained why she wanted to be left alone.

The reasons for Rose's illiteracy were complicated, but the sheer fact of having lost a parent and, as I later learned, having gone through times when her family didn't know where they would live and were short on food, made it difficult if not impossible for her to ask for help. Rose had suffered at least two of what psychologists call adverse childhood experiences (ACEs), which usually result in trauma.[1]

There are many students like Rose in our schools who exhibit difficult behavior or learning challenges as a result of having suffered ACEs. In this chapter, you will learn about the growing body of research about the lasting effects of ACEs, how to think about students whom we label as "difficult" but may very well be suffering the effects of trauma, and how to support these students who are acutely in need. In the second part of the chapter, you will learn about the PAUSE and REACT tool that I've developed for teachers to help struggling students. To start, let's explore what the experts have to say about the critical issue of ACEs in the populations of the students we teach.

A Critical Issue: Adverse Childhood Experiences

A growing body of research has shown that ACEs have become a critical public health issue.[2] ACEs are potentially traumatic experiences and events, ranging from abuse and neglect to living with an adult with a mental illness.

In 2018 the National Survey of Children's Health (NSCH) released data to describe the prevalence of one or more ACEs among children from birth through age 17, as reported by a parent or guardian. More than a third of all children in the US have experienced at least one ACE; the two most common were parental separation or divorce and living with anyone with an alcohol or drug problem. Even more important than exposure to any one specific adverse event is the accumulation of multiple adversities during childhood; unfortunately, 14 percent of children ages 3–17 in the US have experienced two or more ACEs.[3] Although children's responses and their circumstances vary widely, ACEs can have negative lasting effects on health and well-being in childhood or later in life, effects that we often see in students who have difficulty with social-emotional and academic learning.[4] According to the NSCH, the eight most commonly found ACEs are:

- Difficulty covering basics like food or housing somewhat or very often
- Parent or guardian divorced or separated
- Parent or guardian died
- Parent or guardian served time in jail
- Saw or heard parents or other adults slap, hit, kick, or punch in home
- Victim of or witness to violence in neighborhood
- Lived with anyone mentally ill, suicidal, or severely depressed
- Lived with anyone with a problem with alcohol or drugs[5]

The overall risk for ACEs is not shared equally among all students. Disturbingly, Black and Latinx children and youth are more likely to experience ACEs than their White and Asian peers.[6] Discriminatory housing and employment policies, bias in law enforcement and sentencing, and immigration policies have concentrated disadvantage among Black and Latinx students and leave them disproportionately vulnerable to traumatic experiences. Many researchers believe that the chronic experience of racism can itself have toxic effects.[7] Unsafe neighborhoods, unhealthy foster care arrangements, homelessness, and bullying are other examples of chronic stressors that adversely affect students' social and emotional and academic development.

Adverse Childhood Experiences Can Have Profound Effects

ACEs can cause stress reactions that include feelings of intense fear, terror, and helplessness. When activated repeatedly or over a prolonged period of time, toxic levels of stress hormones can interrupt normal physical and mental development and can even change the brain. However, not all students who experience one or even more than one ACE are negatively affected; much depends on the context in which they occur—particularly in the context of positive relationships. This last point is especially important for education leaders. Strong, positive relationships can lessen the adverse effects of ACEs. To learn more about trauma and its effects on students, consider reading Tyrone C. Howard's *All Students Must Thrive.* This book covers many issues with culture, bias, and equity, but Chapter 2 of the book, "How to Create a Trauma-Aware Learning Environment" by Maisah Howard, is particularly helpful. Because of the opportunity to form and nurture strong positive relationships in school with our students, we have a pivotal role to play in how children and young people are affected by trauma.

Triggering Complex Trauma

Complex trauma refers to repeated and prolonged exposure to trauma-inducing situations, usually in a caregiving situation. When a child can't rely on a close caregiver for comfort and safety—whether due to the caregiver's own emotional suffering or because the caregiver is the source of trauma—that young person's ability to metabolize and recover from toxic stress gets seriously hampered.

Joyce Dorado, the cofounder and director of UCSF Healthy Environments and Response to Trauma in Schools (HEARTS), uses the metaphor of a vinyl record to explain the mechanism of complex trauma. Today many of us make playlists to enjoy music, but think of a vinyl record: When a song is played again and again, a groove is worn into the record. If, when playing a different song, someone accidentally knocks the record player, the needle will skip across the record and land in the deepest groove, playing that song yet again. Even when you reach the end of the song, sometimes the groove is so deep the needle skips back to play it once more.

As Joyce explains, complex trauma wears a groove in the brain like a needle on a record turntable. So when something nonthreatening happens that reminds certain students of a traumatic incident, their bodies replay the traumatic reaction—mobilizing them to either run from or fight the threat, while shutting down other systems that help them to think and reason. If this happens over and over, a person becomes more easily triggered into that fear response mode, never giving their body time to recover. A person who has suffered complex trauma in a caregiving relationship and has by necessity adapted to constant triggering can exhibit behavior that can seem crazy or rude when taken out of the context of the original trauma.[8]

For a student in a classroom, complex trauma means that something as simple as the teacher raising his or her voice to get everyone's attention or accidentally getting bumped by another classmate can steer that student into this groove. When triggered, the student's out-of-proportion emotional and sometimes physical reaction often makes no sense to the teacher (or anyone else), making it difficult for the teacher to respond appropriately. As teachers who wish to build caring relationships, we must be alert and sensitive to students who may have difficult or unexpected responses to our best efforts. It may be the case that this student has been hurt in a previous caregiving relationship.

Positive Relationships Help

When you create positive relationships in your classrooms, what do you notice? How do students respond to redirection, change, or other situations throughout your day? Have you ever had a situation with an individual student or students when the strategies did not work? There are many reasons why this might be, and sometimes, it could mean that a student has experienced some type of trauma.

Once you understand the source you can begin to figure out how to help difficult, misbehaving, or withdrawn students. The encouraging news is that

TEACH UP! TIP

Hone Your Trauma-Aware Practices

- Aim to create a family-like classroom and school environment.
- Prioritize student proficiency and growth. This means being flexible with your teaching methods by differentiating learning and assessments for some students.
- Create leadership roles for students both within the classroom and in the school community. This means giving students who may not ordinarily be given an opportunity to lead a chance to demonstrate leadership and responsibility.

trauma exposure does not seal one's fate. There are things that educators and other caring adults can do to mitigate the effects of trauma or toxic stress—and help at-risk students flourish rather than fail. Chief among those things is to establish positive, supportive relationships with all students, including the ones that do not immediately respond as you might wish.

Studies show that students who experience strong and stable relationships with caring adults are better able to regulate their responses to upsetting situations.[9] When we teach students social-emotional skills in connected, compassionate, and vulnerable classrooms, we provide a buffer to ACEs that allow trauma-affected students to become resilient. When trauma-affected students become more self-aware, more socially aware, and more courageous as a result of having allowed to be vulnerable, they are more likely to have positive outcomes in school and in life. The good news is that students who experience ACEs do not necessarily have to indefinitely endure toxic levels of stress.

How to Support Students in Need

The reason I was able to figure out that Rose, my fourth-grader, had not learned to read was because I paid attention to her behavior, asked questions to get to know her, and then did diagnostic testing to determine her reading level. After that, I reached out to the experts in the school, psychologists and reading specialists, so we could find out more about her strengths and weaknesses. I partnered with other teachers to give Rose the job of a helper in one of the kindergarten classrooms at specific parts of the day when the kindergarteners were learning to read. That gave her the opportunity to absorb the phonics and phonemic awareness reading instruction while also setting her up for success to be an older, more responsible class helper. In my class I set up individual stations for Rose to do assignments at her level that looked very different from what I assigned the other students. She also participated in group work, to the best of her ability, with the other fourth-graders so she could have some exposure to concepts appropriate to her age. By the middle of the next year we found Rose a place in another school with a class of about six students and a specially trained teacher who could give her the attention she needed.

I remember the day Rose called me and said, "Ms. Mason, I can read!" She was so excited.

"Read me something, Rose," I said. It really warmed my heart to hear her read from one of her books. It showed me there was nothing "wrong" with Rose. I was right to have assumed the best for her; she'd desperately wanted to learn how to read but didn't know how to find the help. She could learn, but because she'd behaved like a good little girl who was quiet and stayed under the radar, no one had taken the time to build a relationship with her and figure out what was going on.

I've codified the approach I took to help Rose (and many other students) as PAUSE and REACT—a series of steps that you can use with your students who seem out of step or troubled. The next sections explain how the PAUSE and REACT tool works and how others have effectively applied it to students in a variety of situations.

The PAUSE and REACT Tool

With some students, relationships come naturally because of who they are and who you are. Most students naturally gravitate to you if you show interest and care. But with students who have experienced some kind of trauma it's often difficult to crack the nut. What do we do if students do not respond to the culture and strategies we've set up for a relationship-based classroom that emphasizes connection, compassion, and vulnerability?

Pay Attention for signs that a student's behavior or attitude has shifted in a downward direction.

Ask Questions to figure out and determine exactly what is going on for that student.

Use Your Expertise once you have an idea of the student's individual situation to determine if you need to involve other people, such as specialists or parents, to help support the student.

Show Genuine Interest to build trust with a student and to create a space where the student can open up and be honest about what's going on.

Evaluate the Circumstances by taking all of the information you were able to gather and really figure out what's going on and set the best plan of action.

These steps compose a PAUSE.

Once you have figured out a student's individual situation it's time to REACT. This means that you:

Reach Out to create a team for the student that may involve other teachers, coaches, counselors, parents, and so on.

Extend a Helping Hand by doing whatever you can to provide direct support to the student.

Assume the Best for your student by presuming positive intentions; the student wants to learn and become a valued member of the classroom environment.

Create Opportunities for the student inside and outside the classroom where they can feel comfortable and grow.

Tap into Their Greatness by setting the student up for success by building on their interests and strengths.

To see a summary of the acronyms, take a look at Figure 3.1. You'll also find this tool in Appendix 4 and available as a download at www.Leadered .com/TeachUp.

Now that you understand the overview, let's look into each of these steps in more detail and see how teachers have applied them effectively to support individual students.

PAUSE to Find Out What's Going On

PAUSE means taking some time and thought from your usual lesson plans and classroom activities to focus on a student who may be in need of extra support. Although it may seem like more work, *not* taking the time to focus on such students means they will continue to present difficulties in your classroom and potentially become one of the unfortunate societal statistics that we educators are committed to prevent.

Pay Attention

Ultimately and essentially, pause to pay attention to the individual student. Seeing students this way is not rocket science; it's a relatively simple practice but one not practiced often enough. Sometimes the signs that a student is having difficulty are obvious; for example, Mia, a second-grader, is often absent from school and when she does attend frequently uses profanity. Other times, paying attention requires a little sleuthing. For example, a high school math teacher I worked with saw about 140 students per day for relatively short periods of time. How could he pay attention to so many students?

 **Pay Attention**

Look for changes in disposition,
behavior, or habits.

 **Ask Questions**

Uncover the specifics behind why
this change is occurring.
(I noticed...and I'm wondering...?)

 **Use Your Expertise**

Determine if other adults should
be involved.
(school psychologist, principal, parent, etc.)

 Show Genuine Interest

Show the student that their well-being
is important to you.

 Evaluate the Circumstances

Review all of the evidence to determine
a plan of action.

 **Reach Out**

Create a team of support for the student.
(teachers, coaches, counselors, etc.)

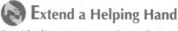 **Extend a Helping Hand**

Provide direct support to the student.

 **Assume the Best**

Presume postitive intentions.

 **Create Opportunities**

Connect the student to opportunities
within and outside of the classroom.

 Tap into Their Greatness

Set the student up for success by building
on their interests and strengths.

Figure 3.1 PAUSE and REACT Tool

When we reviewed his student testing data during one of our coaching conversations, I noticed that one student who usually scored high on assessments had two failing grades and some missing assignments. A little bell went off in my mind when I saw that change in academic performance. When I asked the teacher if he'd noticed anything going on with the student, he paused for a couple of moments to think, then said that this particular student hadn't been hanging around with his usual friend group and had been a little quiet lately.

Ask Questions

Asking questions is a natural and ongoing part of the relationships we build with students. For trauma-affected students, the questions we ask are meant to uncover the specifics of why a particular behavior or change in behavior is occurring. The high school math teacher asked the student, "Hey, I noticed you didn't do well on the last couple of tests. What's going on? Do you need some extra help?" That opens the door to further conversation. The student said, "Oh, my head just wasn't in it that day." That's the cue to ask again. "Really, how come? Was anything bothering you?" Eventually, the teacher learned that the student was being bullied on social media. His friends were posting stuff about him that was embarrassing and rude. Understandably, the student was upset, and that was affecting his study habits and concentration.

You don't always get the answer immediately, so it's important to keep asking until you find out what's really going on. Mia, the second-grader who was using profanity and also being physical with the other students, was acting out because her parents were often fighting at home. Also, the class had switched to a hybrid model which included remote and in-person learning. The teacher began by asking Mia if the remote learning was hard or easy and learned that Mia was frustrated because she kept getting locked out of the computer. "Oh, so you're mad about the computer?" Mia nodded. "It's not only the computer," she added, and then admitted that she didn't want to get on the computer for a class session if her parents were yelling.

Use Your Expertise

Once you've figured out that a student is having problems you don't have to solve the problem alone! Using your expertise means exercising your judgment to determine whether to involve other adults such as the school psychologist, the principal, learning specialists, or parents. For example, after asking permission from the high school student who was bullied on social media, his math teacher reached out to the school counselor to ask for a professional opinion about how to remedy the situation. The counselor had ideas about who might have been doing the bullying and how to talk to those kids. Mia's second-grade teacher reached out to the school counselor and the principal to let them know that Mia was witnessing a lot of conflict and aggression at home, and then she scheduled a meeting with Mia's parents to talk about how their behavior was affecting Mia.

When students are experiencing more serious difficulties, it's especially important to loop in other adult professionals as soon as possible. Lenore was a middle school student who was already failing several classes when she was arrested for theft and possession of narcotics. Her teacher noticed that she was falling asleep and wondered if she might be under the influence during class. After talking to Lenore (who insisted to the teacher that she hadn't stolen anything, but it was all her friend's fault!), the teacher used her expertise to loop in the school psychologist, who could do more of an in-depth assessment and dig deeper into whatever might be going on with Lenore. Although the teacher had done the right thing to pay attention to Lenore's behavior and ask questions, her judgment told her that Lenore's difficulties with the law and drug use were too big for her to handle alone.

Show Genuine Interest

Although you enlist the help of other adults, you're not just passing on responsibility to others for a student who is struggling. To be part of the solution you need to continue to show genuine interest. You need to roll up your sleeves and continue to stay involved! That could mean staying in touch with the other adults and scheduling regular meetings with the counselor or parents to check in and share information on how the student is or is not progressing.

To show genuine interest, you also need to keep paying attention and asking the student questions. If a student's grades have been falling, you want to pay special attention to the next round of exams or homework assignments to see if the student seems to be showing improvement. If a student has been in trouble with the law or drugs, you want to keep talking to show that you are an ally. For example, Lenore's teacher regularly said things like: "I know you're a good kid; you're smart and talented, and you have so much potential. How're you doing?" and to show continued support, she said, "What's going on? How are you doing with your science report?" Working with kids, but especially those who have been affected by trauma, means hanging in there long-term through the downs as well as the ups; that you are willing to do so in and of itself shows genuine interest.

Evaluate the Circumstances

After you have reviewed all the evidence that explains a student's circumstances, you want to determine a plan of action. Reviewing all the evidence means thinking over the conversations you may have had with the student, parents, and other appropriate adults inside and outside the school.

It means collecting data from any diagnostic or psychological diagnostics that the experts may have conducted. Have any written reports been filed? Reviewing the evidence in its entirety is the culmination of the PAUSE and is meant to give you as deep and well-rounded a picture of the student's circumstances as can be. Bear in mind that the picture may include one or more ACEs that have contributed to the student's behavioral or academic difficulties.

Determining a plan of action is likely to involve a team of other adults and your continued support to the student. The plan of action is when you REACT—the subject of the next section in this chapter.

REACT with a Plan to Support Students in Need

Once you have a clear sense of a student's difficulties it's time to REACT by planning and setting in motion the actions and activities that will support the student in moving out of difficulty and into a more productive place where he or she can succeed. REACT is about teamwork and consistency. It means deepening a relationship where you can continue to pay attention and ask questions, but with the goal of checking in with the student, making sure the support plan is ongoing and on track, and making whatever adjustments need to be made along the way.

Reach Out

Once you have a clear picture of the student's circumstances you want to reach out and create a team to support the student. The team is likely to include parents, counselors, and coaches. Some students may already have a history of relationships with one or more of these adults that have lapsed. A student may need to reconnect with a counselor. Or a coach may need to reach out to a student who hasn't been coming to practice.

For example, a high school student named Max was very active in a couple of school sports teams. But when school closed due to the pandemic, Max began to struggle. He neglected his homework; his grades fell; he just wasn't involved. On a video call with one of his teachers, Max admitted he felt depressed. He said he missed the structure and in-person involvement of school. So the teacher reached out to one of the coaches, who called Max. And the coach was able to motivate Max by saying things like, "School is going to be reopening at some point and you want to make sure your grades are up so that when baseball season starts you'll be able to play." Because of the important role he already played in Max's life, the coach was able to help Max get back on track.

Extend a Helping Hand

Even when the student seems to be doing better, it's your job to continue to provide direct support to the student. For example, if a student has been missing online meetings or struggling with technology, you can check in again to see why that's the case and what can be done to remedy the situation. Continue to pay attention and ask questions. "How's it going? What's going on?"

After the coach had talked to Max about keeping up his grades, the teacher extended a helping hand by going over all the missed assignments and setting up new due dates for Max to turn in some of the work he'd been unable to complete. For one of his written assignments, she suggested that he review footage of some professional games and analyze some of the player's moves. When she talked to Max's parents and learned that Max had previously seen a counselor for depression, the teacher suggested that Max make an appointment to see the counselor again. The point is that helping a student who has been struggling is not a one-and-done deal. It requires extending your hand and then keeping your hand in the game.

Assume the Best

Often, students who have suffered one or more ACEs are not used to thinking well of themselves, but as teachers and educators we need to assume the best about them. Every student wants to do well in school. No student wants to be a troublemaker or a failure. When we see students having social-emotional or academic difficulties, chances are that's because there is something stressful going on. For example, the high school math teacher did not jump to the conclusion that the student's grades were dropping because he was lazy. Mia's teacher did not jump to the conclusion that Mia didn't care about school or her classmates because she was swearing and absent from online sessions. Lenore's teacher did not think Lenore was a bad kid because she'd been arrested for shoplifting and using drugs. Max's teacher did not think he was incapable of learning. In each case, the teacher assumed the student was doing the best he or she could under trying circumstances.

Assuming the best also means believing that even the most trauma-affected kids can be helped. We can't give up on our students just because they create difficulty or don't readily conform to the relationship-building strategies we've set up in the classroom. We have to assume that our time with students who have suffered ACEs can help to buffer whatever they have already gone through or whatever stresses they are currently facing in their lives.

Create Opportunities

We tend to take away opportunities from kids when they act out, but often creating opportunities is a much, much more effective way to bring them into relationship with learning and school. You can work with the other adults on the support team to create individual opportunities inside and outside the school. For example, Lenore liked music, so her teacher and the music teacher created an opportunity for Lenore to rewrite the school song and present it at the next school assembly. Because the goal was to keep her from engaging in harmful or self-destructive activities, giving her time and space to use the music room was a way to get her more involved and look forward to coming to school.

Mia, the second-grader who was having difficulty at home with remote learning, loved dance. She was on the dance team at school, and as a result of spending most of the time at home she really missed the after-school rehearsal time with the coach and other dance students. Creating opportunities for Mia meant that her dance coach asked her to record some dance routines for other students to use as a break from sitting in front of the computer all day. Generally speaking, the goal is to create opportunities that will make the student look forward to school in some productive way.

Tap into Their Greatness

Our job as educators is to tap into the greatness that we know every student possesses. Students who have endured one or more ACEs or who are living with toxic stress may not know about their strengths. They may not have received enough positive feedback or praise. They may have gotten the message they are bad, or unlovable, or unable to learn. The goal of PAUSE and REACT is to recognize each student's greatness, and then bring it forth.

Continuing to provide direct support to students with ongoing stress and challenges is one way to tap into greatness. Creating opportunities that set students up for success and enable students to shine is another way to tap into greatness. Ultimately, whatever we can do to establish and nurture strong positive relationships as an adult who supports and believes in the student will bring forth that greatness.

Additional Strategies

Here are additional strategies to be used in conjunction with the PAUSE and REACT tool. When you notice that a student is having a difficult time, start by asking yourself, "What's happening here?" rather than "What's wrong with this student?" This simple mindset shift can help you realize that the student has been triggered into a fear response, which can take many forms.

Be aware that not all students will act out. However, for those who do, once you recognize the trigger, kindly and compassionately reflect back to the student: "I see that you're having trouble with this problem," or "You seem like you're getting kind of irritated," and then offer a couple of choices of things the student can do. This will help the student gain a sense of control and agency and help him or her to feel safe. Over time, if a student who is experiencing something that is frightening or harmful sees that you really care and understand, then he or she will be more likely to say, "I need help."

Create Calm, Predictable Transitions

Transitions between activities can easily trigger a student into survival mode. That feeling of "uh oh, what's going to happen next?" can be highly associated with a situation at home where, for example, a student's happy, loving parent can, without warning, turn into a monster after having too much to drink.

Some teachers will play music or ring a meditation bell or blow a harmonica to signal it's time to transition. The important thing is to build a routine around transitions so that students know what the transition is going to look like, what they're supposed to be doing, and what's next.

Praise Publicly, Criticize Privately

For students who have experienced complex trauma, getting in trouble can sometimes mean either they or a family member will get hit. And for others, "I made a mistake" can mean "I'm entirely unlovable." To counteract these tendencies, teachers need to be particularly sensitive when reprimanding or criticizing these students.

Capture those moments when the student is doing really well and point it out to build his confidence: "Wow, I love how well you are working with your group," or "Thank you for helping your classmate." When you need to redirect the behavior, do so privately and in as calm a voice as possible.

Adopt and Adapt a Mindfulness Practice in Your Classroom

Mindfulness is a fabulous tool for counteracting the impact of trauma. However, it can also be threatening for students who have experienced trauma, as the practice may bring up scary and painful emotions and body sensations. If you incorporate mindfulness in your classroom, consider using the following adaptations created by the UCSF HEARTS program and Mindful Schools (https://hearts.ucsf.edu/resources):

- Tell students they can close their eyes at the beginning of the practice. Or they should look at a spot in front of them so that no one feels stared at.
- Instead of focusing on how the body feels, have students focus on a ball or other object they're holding in their hands—what it feels like and looks like in their palm.
- Focus on the sounds in the room or of cars passing outside the classroom—something external to the body.

By breaking mindfulness practice down into these elemental components, the student is more likely to have a successful experience—and thus be more willing to practice in the future.

Take Care of Yourself

With so much focus placed on building relationships and developing students' social-emotional learning, it can be difficult to remember to care for yourself. But you also need to attend to your own social-emotional well-being. Are you becoming overly tired? How do you prevent yourself from being stressed, anxious, worn down, or burnt out? What can you do to help yourself relax? You may need mindful minutes. Making time for hobbies or activities for fun and relaxation is important self-care that helps you recharge so you can be at your best for your students. The metaphor of putting on your own oxygen mask first before putting it on the child is very true in this situation.

Teach Up! For Strong Relationships

So far in this book, I have introduced you to the important foundational pieces for building a relationship-based classroom and provided you with strategies to help students feel safe enough to be themselves, learn joyously, and practice connection, compassion, and vulnerability. In this chapter, you've learned about the prevalence of ACEs and their effects on students in your classroom as well as extra steps or special strategies that can help build the positive relationships that trauma-affected students so need, strong relationships that can help our students flourish in school and in their futures. Later in this book, I will discuss how you combine the Relationships Rubric with the Rigor/Relevance Framework to create truly exciting learning experiences for your students.

TEACH UP! TIP

Draft a Self-Care Plan

No one knows you better than yourself. When you're starting to have more challenging days and perhaps are feeling more on edge in the classroom and at home, it's time to activate your self-care plan. Activities that bring you joy are key to self-care. While we'd all love a vacation to Aruba, something simple can also work wonders to help us reset. Here are some of my self-care plan activities: cleaning out my purse, getting a massage, taking a spa day, quality time with my family, getting away from my family, playing tennis, gym time, cooking, listening to my favorite podcasts, escaping into a book.

KEY TAKEAWAYS

- Nearly half of all children in the US have experienced at least one ACE; the two most common are economic hardship and parental separation or divorce. Even more important than exposure to any one specific adverse event is the accumulation of multiple adversities during childhood; unfortunately, one in ten children in the US have experienced three or more ACEs.

- ACEs can cause stress reactions, including feelings of intense fear, terror, and helplessness. When activated repeatedly or over a prolonged period of time, toxic levels of stress hormones can interrupt normal physical and mental development and can even change the brain.

- Helping a student who has experienced trauma or toxic stress does not mean treating the consequences directly but is instead about interacting in ways that help students form strong, positive relationships. As educators we can play a vital role to help students to become resilient and even flourish.

- When you notice that a student is having a difficult time, start by asking yourself, "What's happening here?" rather than "What's wrong with this student?"

- PAUSE requires you to Pay attention, Ask Questions, Use Your Expertise, Show Genuine Interest, and Evaluate the Circumstances. In doing so, you establish or deepen a relationship with a trauma-affected student by showing that you care, reaching out to other adults, and figuring out what's really going on.

- REACT requires you to Reach Out to a team for continued support for the student. The team could be other teaches, coaches, counselors, and parents. Continuing your relationship with the trauma-affected student means that you Extend a Helping Hand, Assume the Best, Create Opportunities for the student, and Tap into Their Greatness to set students up for success by building on their interests and strengths.

The Four Quadrants of Learning

A dedicated middle school teacher in Missouri named Gwen seemed to have done everything right yet was displeased with her evaluations. What could be wrong? When I observed her teaching, I saw well-behaved students at their desks carefully completing worksheets. The desks were arranged in neat pods, the classroom space was well organized, and the walls were decorated with posters of student work. If a student had a question, he raised his hand and Gwen came over to quietly confer or offer explanation. Several times I saw students smilingly thank Gwen for her help; she was warm and personable and seemed to genuinely care for them as individuals. At the end of the lesson, Gwen collected the assignments and reminded students of the night's homework, which was also displayed on the screen in the front of the classroom. When the bell rang, the students obediently packed up their things and filed quietly out of the room.

Given this evidence of having done everything right, why was Gwen displeased with her teaching evaluations? Why was she not meeting her district's achievement expectations? Although her students were compliant, several parents had complained that their kids were bored and not sufficiently challenged. They found the assignments and worksheets overly tedious.

The problem, as she realized in further coaching sessions, was that despite her best intentions, Gwen did not yet understand the Rigor/Relevance Framework for curriculum design and instruction. Too much low-level work without connections to authentic real-world tasks do indeed keep learning from becoming the dynamic and engaging experience it can be. Gwen wanted the best for her students; but she didn't yet have the understanding or support to teach up in ways that not only satisfy district requirements but also prepare students for the world into which they will graduate.

In the first three chapters, we discussed the crucial need for relationship building and strategies for creating learning environments that are based on connection, compassion, and vulnerability. You learned about the tremendous impact that strong, positive relationships have on all students while they are in school and for their future as productive members of society, especially if students have suffered trauma or toxic stress. Think of relationships as the soil that nurtures students as they grow academically. Relationships are vitally important for their own sake, but they are also the foundation for establishing rigor and relevance.

In the next couple of chapters we move on to discuss the various facets of the Rigor/Relevance Framework and how it ignites learning. Later chapters will go into the specifics of how to plan and implement lessons that encompass rigor and relevance, but this chapter will take you through the theoretical scaffolding to explain the "what" of the framework. You will learn about the six levels that make up the Knowledge Taxonomy, the five levels in the Application Model, and the Four Learning Quadrants. That may sound like a lot to cover, but I'll explain each one separately in the first part of the chapter and then go on to show you what it means to put them all together. Let's get started!

The Rigor/Relevance Framework

The Rigor/Relevance Framework, shown in Figure 4.1, is a tool developed by the International Center for Leadership in Education (ICLE) to examine curriculum, instruction, and assessment.

A reproducible version of the Rigor/Relevance Framework is provided in Appendix 5, as well as available for download at www.Leadered.com/TeachUp. The Rigor/Relevance Framework is based on the two dimensions of higher standards and student achievement. Those two dimensions are the Knowledge Taxonomy and the Application Model. Let's look briefly at each dimension in turn and then evaluate how they work.

The Knowledge Taxonomy for Rigor

The continuum of knowledge describes the increasingly complex ways in which we think. Adapted from Bloom's taxonomy, the Knowledge Taxonomy

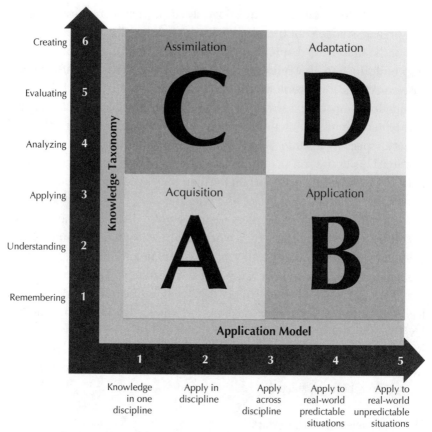

Figure 4.1 **The Rigor/Relevance Framework**

provides a common language for teachers to discuss and exchange learning and assessment methods. We can map six levels of rigor:

1. Remembering
2. Understanding
3. Applying
4. Analyzing
5. Evaluating
6. Creating

The low end of this continuum involves acquiring knowledge and being able to recall or locate that knowledge in a simple manner. Memorizing how to spell and correctly pronounce a list of vocabulary words is an example of the first level. Understanding what the words mean and how to use them in a sentence is level two knowledge. Applying those words in a sentence to demonstrate their correct meaning is an example of level three. Analyzing and evaluating a story in which those words appear occurs in levels four and five. Creating a story using the vocabulary words and writing them down is level six knowledge.

As you can see, the higher end of the Knowledge Taxonomy labels more complex ways in which we use knowledge. At this level, knowledge is fully integrated into our mind, and we can take several pieces of knowledge and combine them in both logical and creative ways. More generally speaking, when using higher-order thinking a student can solve multistep problems, create unique work, and devise solutions.

The rigor levels of the Knowledge Taxonomy can be used either to intentionally create lessons at the different levels or to evaluate the level of rigor in existing curriculum, instruction, or assessment.

The Application Model for Relevance

The second continuum, created by ICLE founder Dr. Bill Daggett, is known as the Application Model and pertains to relevance. The five levels of this continuum are:

1. Knowledge in one discipline
2. Application in one discipline
3. Application across disciplines
4. Application to real-world predictable situations
5. Application to real-world unpredictable situations

The Application Model describes a continuum of ways that we use knowledge to add relevance to instruction. While the low end is knowledge acquired for its own sake, the high end signifies action, or using that knowledge to solve complex real-world problems, and create projects, designs, and other works for use in real-world situations. The Application Model is also key to intentional planning or evaluating the level of relevance in curriculum, instruction, or assessment.

The Four Quadrants

The Rigor/Relevance Framework has four quadrants. The Knowledge Taxonomy runs vertically, with the lowest knowledge levels of rigor in the bottom quadrants and the higher levels in the top quadrants. The Application Model runs horizontally across the quadrants, with the least amount of relevance at the left and the most on the right. In my coaching sessions with teachers, we often spend time looking closely at each of the quadrants to examine what it means to match up rigor and relevance at differing levels.

The Rigor/Relevance Framework, as represented in Figure 4.1, gives us a common language and tool to think and talk about what we expect students to learn and how we design our teaching. The beauty of the model is its versatility—there are myriad ways to combine the knowledge levels and application models for varying types of rigor and relevance. The quadrants pull together the rigor and relevance dimensions.

- Quadrant A represents simple recall and basic application of knowledge.
- Quadrant B represents applying the knowledge across a variety of situations.
- Quadrant C represents more complex thinking but without a broader context and in one discipline.
- Quadrant D embraces higher levels of knowledge and their application to real-world, unpredictable situations that involve more than one discipline.

Note that Quadrants B and D are based on action or high degrees of application. Applying knowledge from a variety of sources to solve complex problems and create real-world products are types of Quadrant D learning. Although I'll introduce Quadrant D learning in this chapter, Chapter 6, which is primarily focused on Quadrant D learning, goes into more depth

TEACH UP! TIP

Focus on All the Quadrants

Good instruction means developing lessons in each of the four quadrants. I've found that oftentimes administrators are hyperfocused on Quadrant D learning, and feel they should always see that type of learning in their teacher's classrooms. However, learning is best done across the quadrants.

and detail. Keep in mind that no one quadrant is "better" than the others. However, in my coaching experience I have noticed that many lessons tend to land in Quadrant A without reaching the other quadrants in the framework. The important thing to remember is that good instruction means developing lessons in each of the four quadrants to provide students with the appropriate amount of scaffolding and experience with complex and authentic learning tasks.

Now let's describe each of the four quadrants more expansively, with examples to illustrate how each quadrant might look in the classroom.

Quadrant A — Acquisition

In Quadrant A learning, students gather and store bits of knowledge and information. Students are primarily expected to remember or understand this acquired knowledge. In Quadrant A activities student may calculate, identify, list, match, memorize, recall, recite, and spell.

Examples of acquisition include memorizing multiplication tables or learning the names of the 50 states in the United States. Quadrant A learning can be taken to a higher level if, for example, students list the states' names in alphabetical order or calculate how many individual socks it would take to clothe every person in their classroom. There's plenty of value in Quadrant A—it isn't necessarily "bad" or "wrong," as long as students don't spend all their learning time simply acquiring facts.

Quadrant B — Application

In Quadrant B learning, students use acquired knowledge to solve problems, design solutions, and complete work. Other Quadrant B learning activities include assignments in which they collect, draw, follow, illustrate, look up, measure, practice, operate, role play, and solve.

For example, in Quadrant B, students can look up the history of a specific US state and determine the natural resources that have a major impact on the local economy. They can measure how many gallons of paint it might take to paint the classroom. More advanced Quadrant B learning activities might include creating a visual representation of a state's natural resources in connection with the population or using the details in an anchor text to set up a multiplication word problem.

Quadrant C — Assimilation

Students extend and refine their acquired knowledge to analyze and solve problems as well as create unique solutions. Quadrant C activities may ask students to cite, classify, compare, contrast, debate, diagram, differentiate, evaluate, explain, generate, infer, prove, research, and summarize.

In Quadrant C, students might compare and contrast attributes of different states or generate questions for what they want to know about their subject. They might infer how many gallons it would take to paint a second classroom in the building or explain the steps in the process they used to solve a multiplication problem.

Quadrant D — Adaptation

Students in every grade have the competence to think in complex ways and apply knowledge and skills they have acquired. Even when confronted with perplexing unknowns, students are able to use extensive knowledge and skill to create solutions and take action that further develops their skills and knowledge. In Quadrant D activities students will argue, conclude, create, discover, invent, predict, prioritize, propose, revise, and teach.

As an educator and a coach I have found the Rigor/Relevance Framework to be a powerful and effective resource for teachers around instructional planning and assessment. It is based on traditional elements of education yet allows plenty of room for individual interpretation and creativity. The framework is relatively easy to understand and flexible enough to be used at any grade level and in many learning environments. Some districts have even found its structure serves as a bridge between the school and the community. Most importantly, it offers a common language and set of ideas that we can use to talk about creating more rigorous and relevant instruction to teach up to our students. Rigor and relevance, when rooted in relationships, promise to provide all our students an education that will stand them in good stead after graduation and beyond.

Defining Rigor

Rigor refers to academic rigor — learning in which students demonstrate a thorough, in-depth mastery of challenging tasks to develop cognitive skills through reflective thought, analysis, problem solving, evaluation, or creativity. Rigorous learning can and should occur at all grade levels and in every subject area.

Here's what rigor is *not*: more homework, more worksheets, moving more quickly through materials, highest level reading groups, and AP or Honors classes. Instead, rigor means framing curriculum to provide students with learning experiences at the higher levels of the Knowledge Taxonomy. Rigor is all about the quality and nature of thinking in which our students engage. When we teach up for rigor, we train our students to become the citizens of the future who will solve problems, innovate, invent, and create.

Defining Relevance

It's easy to confuse relevance in the learning framework with a relevant topic that can serve as a kind of hook to get students interested in learning. Relevance is not about assigning a sports enthusiast to read a book about soccer. It's not about suggesting that a student who likes the ocean write a research report about whales. Sure, that approach can help a student connect to an assignment, but they are not the same thing as relevance. Instead, relevance describes two dimensions of learning:

- Applying core knowledge, concepts, or skills to solve authentic, real-world problems
- Interdisciplinary and contextual learning

Student work engaging relevance can range from routine to complex at any grade and in any subject. Relevant learning is most often created through authentic problems or tasks, simulation, service learning, connecting concepts to current issues, and teaching others. For example, if students are tasked with measuring the length and width of a rectangle, they are applying their knowledge in one discipline which has a low level of relevance. However, if they also spend time analyzing how visual artists have represented rooms using rectangles and then create an original design based on the analysis, the task becomes interdisciplinary, including math and art, and thus the level of relevance increases.

The Need for More Rigorous and Relevant Instruction

Mark Lobosco, vice president of Talent Solutions at LinkedIn, spoke to what many of today's employers are looking for when they hire. When asked about the qualities needed from employees, Lobosco answered, "Not only their technical skills, but also their ability to think creatively, collaborate effectively, and adapt quickly."[1] Unfortunately, too many of our students are not prepared to fulfill these workforce requirements. In the most recent LinkedIn Top Skills list, the top five most needed skills were creativity, persuasion, collaboration, adaptability, and time management.[2] In addition, the McKinsey group studied the changes in work requirements between now and 2030.[3] To identify these new requirements, they surveyed 100 small companies, 100 medium-sized companies, and 100 large companies. Figure 4.2 shows a breakdown of their results.

As the figure shows, there will be a 15 percent decline in the need for basic cognitive skills and a 14 percent decline in manual and physical skills. These two skills categories—on the left side of the figure—are where we spent almost all of our time and resources in our schools during the last few decades. What skills will students need to thrive in the future? Higher cognitive skills, social and emotional skills, and technological skills.

So how do we create more opportunities for students to be able to practice these types of skills so that they are ready for the future workplace?

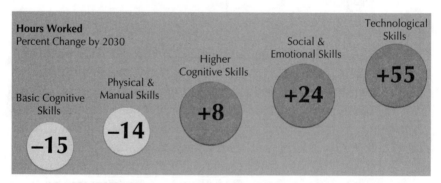

Hours Worked
Percent Change by 2030

Basic Cognitive Skills **−15**

Physical & Manual Skills **−14**

Higher Cognitive Skills **+8**

Social & Emotional Skills **+24**

Technological Skills **+55**

Figure 4.2 Skills for the Future
Source: Adapted from Bughin et al., "Skill Shift: Automation and the Future of the Workforce," McKinsey Global Institute, May 23, 2018. Retrieved from https://www.mckinsey.com/featured-insights/future-of-work/skill-shift-automation-and-the-future-of-the-workforce.

How can we use resources to help our students have more rigorous experiences that will prepare them for future jobs and the future world?

As you've probably noticed, a lot of these new requirements include social skills like persuasion and collaboration. Persuasion and collaboration may not necessarily be built into our standards, but they are critical skills to develop because we know that colleges and workplaces increasingly expect students to feel comfortable working productively with others.

Agility is another important proficiency to develop. When change occurs, we need to figure out what to do to keep up or adapt. The sudden switch to remote learning or hybrid learning that so many of us experienced required plenty of agility! We were required to take chances with new ways of teaching, to think outside the box, and to take the initiative. All these proficiencies are important for our students in school and in their future endeavors.

Today's kids are not doing a whole lot of talking. They play a lot of video games. They spend too much time on social media. They text very short messages that often use emoji as stand-ins for nuanced or complex responses. And so now more than ever, we need to provide our students with opportunities to practice their oral and written communication. Because once they get to college—and beyond—they will be required to communicate ideas, be persuasive, help people, analyze problems, and ask for information.

We live in the information age. We—and our students—can access more information and data on the internet than the previous generation could access in a lifetime. Think, for example, of how much information school districts now have about students. The problem is, how do we manage, analyze, and productively use these ever increasing amounts of information?

Imagination and curiosity are essential. The more we can instill and cultivate these qualities in our students, the more likely they are to become engaged learners who can think innovatively and help find solutions to the enormous problems in the world. When we think of our job as educators, we need to consider how we are preparing students for an uncertain and rapidly evolving future.

Teaching Students the Rigor/Relevance Framework

If you are reluctant to talk with students about the Rigor/Relevance Framework, know that students are totally capable of understanding its different levels and dimensions and the role that each quadrant can play in their learning. Teachers have found that students can be one of the strongest advocates for increasing rigor and relevance. Talking with them about the framework not only strengthens your relationship but also provides a learning experience that encourages analysis, evaluation, and self-reflection. In general, students are hungry for learning that is relevant and become more engaged when it's included in the curriculum. Students also like to be challenged in meaningful ways and gain confidence when they meet those challenges through effort and persistence.

I suggest sharing with students the Rigor/Relevance Framework—either Figure 4.1, descriptions, or both—and ask them to reflect on learning experiences that fit within the various quadrants. Sharing the language of each of the dimensions also gives students the tools to talk about learning. Students are usually quick to figure out how their teachers "operate," and it's a good idea for them to be aware that the strategies you use and the role you play as a teacher changes as you move into higher levels of rigor and relevance. Likewise, they can become aware that their work and responsibilities will change at higher levels of rigor and relevance. If students understand the framework and levels of instruction, they are often more easily motivated to complete the work demanded by high-rigor/high-relevance learning.

Standards and the Rigor/Relevance Framework

Unfortunately, the statistics about students and standards are grim. When assessing college readiness in 2015, the 12th grade National Assessment of Education Progress (NAEP) released data that only 25 percent of students tested at proficient or above in math, and 37 percent of students tested at proficient or above in reading.[4] That means three quarters of students tested below proficient in math and over half tested below proficient in reading. As educators, we clearly need to do better! The Rigor/Relevance Framework is designed to raise these student proficiencies.

The standards movement of the past several decades has caused teachers to shift from thinking about curriculum as a list of content knowledge (multiplication, cause and effect, ancient civilizations, and so on) to a description of knowledge that students must demonstrate. Standards can be useful and on the positive side have created consensus around high expectations for students.

When teachers begin to teach to a standard, they may think the best approach is, "Here is the knowledge, let me demonstrate or explain, then I'll have the student practice it." That's the rationale behind all those worksheets. Students can and do learn from watching and practicing. However, students become bored if your instructional routine always takes this form. Students often see little value in it and are therefore likely to become passively compliant but complaining or noncompliant and failing. Neither of these outcomes is desirable! The problem often stems from the fact that standardized tests pressure teachers to prepare students in recalling the information required to answer largely low-rigor and low-relevance test questions, reinforcing this routine, direct instruction.

However, standards don't limit the level of rigor and relevance in instruction. It is up to the teacher to define the appropriate levels. The secret to more successful testing outcomes is this: when students have the chance to demonstrate learning at higher levels of rigor and relevance, they learn standards more deeply, retain the learning longer, and become more engaged in learning. When it comes time to fill in the bubbles or write short-answer responses on a standardized test, they are more likely to supply the correct answer.

In practical terms, how can the Rigor/Relevance Framework be used as a guide to teach standards? Consider a commonly used middle-level geometry standard that directs: "Have students examine the congruence, similarity, and line or rotational symmetry of objects using transformations." Here are a few examples that show a range of assignments that a teacher might choose to teach this standard—by no stretch of the imagination are these examples exhaustive.

- Quadrant A: Students sort and label objects in the classroom that are symmetrical.
- Quadrant B: Students make observations of symmetry in nature.
- Quadrant C: Groups of students are asked to modify a pair of algebraic expressions so that when they are plotted they show symmetry.
- Quadrant D: Students are given a robot and are asked to program the robot so it moves in a symmetrical manner to complete a function.

No doubt you could come up with plenty of other application examples for your classroom! The point is that each of these learning experiences is based on the same standard—to understand symmetry—but the level of rigor and relevance vary widely depending on the quadrant the learning falls into. Each lesson leads students to very different types of learning experiences and engagements. Again, if students have learned to apply geometry or other math concepts deeply via challenges that encompass rigor and relevance, answering low-level questions on a test is just one more challenge that they can meet, most often with success. Teaching up to high rigor and high relevance is a more engaged, deeper, and ultimately more successful way for more students to meet higher standards.

Strategies to Increase Rigor and Relevance

You can use many different paths to increase rigor and relevance in your instruction. Depending on your classroom situation and your comfort level with the Rigor/Relevance Framework, you may want to choose one of the basic pathways listed below. Again, this is not an exhaustive list—there are many choices!

1. Add a High-Rigor and High-Relevance Performance Task

Most teachers modify existing lessons to increase the level of rigor and relevance. You can begin by considering the instructional outcomes or standards for a particular unit and then include a high-rigor and high-relevance performance task as an activity for students to demonstrate their learning, usually at the end of the unit. A carefully constructed performance task naturally leads teachers to raise the rigor and relevance of instruction, thus increasing student achievement.

2. Change Instructional Moves

Teachers have many choices for how to structure a lesson. Know that lecture and worksheets correlate with low rigor and low relevance while project design, problem-based learning, and student presentation correlate with high rigor and high relevance. Mix them up.

3. Change Assessments

A simple way to raise the level of rigor and relevance is to assess in ways that do more than simply ask students to recall answers. An assessment that asks students to think as well as more fully explain and demonstrate their knowledge will organically raise the level of rigor and relevance.

4. Make Instruction Interdisciplinary

Move beyond the boundaries of one instructional area. Typically, secondary instruction is very focused on one instructional area, but elementary-level teachers also tend to focus on one instructional strand. As teachers increase relevance, the boundaries between disciplines typically disappear. Another approach to increasing rigor and relevance is to combine learning standards from several different disciplines into a single learning experience. An excellent strategy for making instruction more interdisciplinary is for core teachers to integrate the arts and career and technical education within their instruction.

Beyond Worksheets: Bump It Up!

By now you can see how the Rigor/Relevance Framework raises classroom engagement and learning beyond the passivity experienced by students who sit quietly at their desks and complete worksheets. Gwen, whom you met at the beginning of this chapter, was able to make some major adjustments to her instruction to incorporate rigor and relevance. We call this "bumping it up." After I observed her class, we debriefed and talked about her understanding of the framework and her teaching goals. Soon she was able to plan using the four quadrants in ways that allowed her to increase the level of rigor and relevance in her lessons to give her students opportunities to sharpen their critical thinking skills in engaging ways. Yes, her students still used worksheets for some learning in Quadrant A, but they were also exposed to real-world authentic tasks. I have coached many teachers like Gwen in school districts across the country both affluent and underserved. Again and again, I have seen that incorporating the Rigor/Relevance Framework has opened the door to nearly limitless opportunities for student learning experiences, the ones that stimulate and engage for better outcomes in school and as future citizens.

In the Chapter 5 you will learn more about how to define and implement appropriate levels of rigor and relevance in your classroom. I will take you through the practicalities of using the Rigor/Relevance Framework for curriculum planning, classroom instructing, and student assessing.

KEY TAKEAWAYS

- The Rigor/Relevance Framework is a tool developed by the International Center for Leadership in Education (ICLE) to examine curriculum, instruction, and assessment. The Rigor/Relevance Framework is based on the two dimensions of higher standards and student achievement. Those two dimensions are the Knowledge Taxonomy and the Application Model.

- The Knowledge Taxonomy has six levels: (1) remembering, (2) understanding, (3) applying, (4) analyzing, (5) evaluating, and (6) creating. Thinking moves from simple to more complex as it moves higher up knowledge levels.

- The Application Model has five levels: (1) knowledge in one discipline, (2) application in one discipline, (3) application across disciplines, (4) application to real-world predictable situations, and (5) application to real-world unpredictable situations. Students become more engaged when their learning has applications.

- The four quadrants are where rigor and relevance intersect to create defined learning experiences. Good instruction draws from each of the four quadrants.

- Rigorous learning occurs when students demonstrate a thorough, in-depth mastery of challenging tasks to develop cognitive skills through reflective thought, analysis, problem solving, evaluation, or creativity.

- Relevant learning is most often created through authentic problems or tasks, simulation, service learning, connecting concepts to current issues, and teaching others. Relevance can range from routine to complex at any grade and in any subject.

- When students demonstrate learning at higher levels of rigor and relevance, they learn standards more deeply, retain the learning longer, become more engaged in learning, and testing outcomes are likely to improve.

5

Instruction for Today's Classrooms

Cliff was an elementary school teacher in Georgia who wanted to help his students rise above the low district test scores in ELA and math. He was aware that the tasks he assigned were not as rigorous or as engaging as they could be, but because his students were struggling he didn't believe they could handle anything more challenging before they had mastered basic skills. One day, as part of a coaching program I was leading, he visited a colleague's classroom. There, the students were engaged in small-group tasks; unlike in Cliff's classroom, where students often seemed discouraged, in his colleague's classroom everyone seemed to be a proud and eager learner. One group was programming robots. Another group was editing a class newsletter. "How can I motivate my students?" Cliff asked me during our next one-on-one coaching session. "I would love for my kids to be learning at that level, but they're still trying to get up to speed with basic stuff."

In the weeks that followed, Cliff learned to create instructional tasks that made learning more rigorous and relevant. He learned to bump up some of the very basic skill set exercises to include higher-level thinking. He engaged students' creativity and got them involved in projects that had real-world applications. What's more, his students scored higher on district and state-level standards-based tests.

Chapter 4 described the "what" of the Rigor/Relevance Framework and how incorporating knowledge levels and various kinds of relevancies are crucial for creating authentic and engaged learning experiences that set high expectations for students. In this chapter, like Cliff in my opening story, you will learn about the "how" of applying the framework to your teaching to better integrate instructional tasks from each of the four

Rigor/Relevance quadrants. You will learn about the relationships between assessment and instruction, how to draw from more than one subject to make your student learning interdisciplinary, and the role of technology in the Rigor/Relevance Framework. I will discuss learning in all four quadrants and also demonstrate how to "bump up" a learning task from one quadrant to the next, increasing the level of rigor and relevance as you go.

Planning for Rigor and Relevance

Instructional planning is often divided into three components: curriculum, instruction, and assessment. Curriculum is what students learn, instruction is how students learn, and assessment is in what way and how well students are expected to demonstrate what they have learned as a result of the instruction. Traditionally, these three elements have been approached as three separate steps, one following the other. Many teachers learned to plan their lessons using this linear model: decide what to teach, design how to teach it, and then determine how to measure student achievement.

Teaching that follows this traditional planning model is also often linear. Topics are introduced sequentially, with periodic pauses for a chapter or unit test that determines how well students have learned. At the secondary level, where content is rich and takes priority, instructional planning especially tends to focus on the pacing. Teachers and students often feel pressured to keep up with a predetermined list of topics that must be covered during the course of a semester. In this model, which can be described as "teach it, test it, lose it," teaching becomes all about "coverage." The problem is that this model fails to emphasize student learning and lacks characteristics that lead to the rigorous and relevant engaged learning students need to not only improve test scores but also to do well in college and beyond.

The Rigor/Relevance Framework follows the recent research and innovations in education that find the three elements—curriculum, instruction, and assessment—are not separate and linear, but are instead interrelated. In the new model, planning becomes a question of dynamically linking all three components. Instruction and assessment have significant overlap, and authentic assessment occurs more naturally as part of the instructional process. Student learning becomes the result of facilitated instructional experiences and assessments. Let's look at how this can work.

Begin with the Outcome

In my coaching capacities, I travel from my home in Atlanta to cities and states all over the US. When I am assigned to a school in a distant location, I need to plan my trip. If traveling by air, I need to find out the answer to many questions. Which flight should I book? Do I need a rental car? Where will I stay during my visit? And so on. Traveling by car entails an entirely different set of concerns. What route should I take? How much gas do I need? Regardless, when planning a trip, I always begin with my end destination and then I plan backward for how I can reach that particular destination.

Planning for rigor and relevance also begins with the end destination. Sometimes referred to as "backward design,"[1] the model asks teachers to begin with the outcome or standards students are to learn and then to map out the assessment and instructional tasks that will enable students to reach that standard. Rather than thinking in terms of a series of activities or how best to cover a topic, backward design may be thought of as purposeful task analysis: Given a task to be accomplished, how do we get there? What kinds of lessons and practices are needed to master key performances?

This backward approach to curricular design also departs from another common practice: thinking about assessment as something to plan *after* teaching is completed. Rather than creating assessments near the conclusion of a unit of study (or relying on premade tests, which may not assess state standards completely or appropriately), backward design calls for teachers to think about the work students will produce and how it might be assessed as they begin to plan.

Standards-Driven Curriculum

What's unique about ICLE's approach to curriculum is that it is a standards-driven approach that enables educators to design for and monitor student progress. Curriculum is not an end-in-itself, but rather a means to an end: student mastery of standards through authentic learning experiences that access the four learning quadrants. Curriculum planning asks you to think broadly about what standards you will teach throughout the school year, what resources are available, and what each level of learning looks like in each of the four quadrants. As Larry Ainsworth and Kyra Donovan wrote in their bestselling book, *Rigorous Curriculum Design*, "For educators to meet the challenging learning needs of students—comprehend all the standards, prepare for a variety of formative and summative assessments, and demonstrate proficiency on high-stakes external exams—they must have a clear road map to follow throughout the school year."[2]

You may find yourself on a curriculum writing team or have your curriculum provided to you by the district, but keep in mind that if you receive a set curriculum, you may still want to customize or tailor it based on individual needs of your students.

Product and Performance Assessments

In the Rigor/Relevance Framework, instruction and assessment often occur together. This means that it's best to consider assessment before planning instruction. An assessment is where students demonstrate understanding, knowledge, and skills; there are many types, and no type is better than another. The important thing is to choose an assessment type that matches the student work. For example, if the work involves recalling a body of knowledge (Quadrant A), a multiple-choice or short-answer test may be fine. If the work involves designing or creating something new in response to a real-world problem (Quadrant D), a presentation is probably more appropriate.

Assessments generally fall into two categories: product or performance. A product is a tangible item that students turn in for you to assess: a report, an essay, a paper, a test, or a slide deck. A performance is a time-based experience that students do to demonstrate learning and is usually a vehicle for students to be active and talking. Performance assessments may include a debate, a presentation of their findings to a local council, a video news broadcast, or an audio poem.

By using the Rigor/Relevance Framework in this planning step, a teacher can develop appropriate levels of instruction more accurately.

TEACH UP! TIP

End the Work with Meaning

Student activity without an end product or performance in mind is often busy work. Instruction, no matter how engaging or intellectual, is only beneficial if it ends with students demonstrating their knowledge and using their skills from the learning experience.

Designating high-rigor assessments in Quadrants C or D requires instruction that supports high-level thinking skills. Product and performance tasks can be positioned at different levels of rigor or relevance. For example, when an expectation is set of real-world application by designating Quadrants B or D on the framework, a conscious commitment is made to work toward real-world application.

Instruction: What Students Do

In my coaching career I have found that teachers often spend a lot of time and thought figuring out what they need to do to prepare for and deliver a lesson, but sometimes focus less on what it is that students actually do. I once visited a high school English class that met for a 90-minute block. The students were divided into groups and given questions about a novel the class had recently read and then were expected to regroup with the larger class and report back on the individual discussions for the last 30 minutes of the class. The problem was that each small group was given only one question to discuss! As you can imagine, the students used what amounted to free time to chitchat or do work for other classes. Had the teacher assigned each small group additional questions or asked them, for example, to collaborate on writing a short essay-response during the allotted time, she would have planned for a more rigorous learning experience.

Using the four quadrants to gauge the rigor and relevance of the instructional tasks is a way to ensure that you are on track to truly teach the standards. It can take a little practice to make sure your instructional tasks align up correctly and that your intentions match up with your actions. For example, if you've assigned students a Quad C task but upon closer examination find out that it's really a Quad A task, the problem is that you have not exposed your students to rigorous content. You can learn to tweak or enhance your initial instructional task so that it falls more solidly into the rigor expected of the C or D quadrant. Instead of asking students to make *observations about how* the protagonist changed throughout the story (Quad A task), bump up the assignment by asking students to *analyze why* the protagonist changed (Quad C task). Unless students have sufficient experience with the level of rigor that's embedded in the standards, they are unlikely to do well on low- or high-stake assessments.

On the other hand, if you find that you are assigning students instructional activities that are only in Quad C and Quad D, your students may be struggling academically because you have not exposed them to the low-rigor tasks upon which they can scaffold and build to be able to complete the more challenging tasks of the upper quadrants. Students will have a hard time developing a proposal for how to use a new community space (Quad D task) unless they have a solid understanding of its actual size, community needs, and city funding allocation (Quad A tasks.) Once you have a sense of where individual instructional tasks fall you will become much more intentional about exposing your students to learning at varied levels of rigor and relevance.

Interdisciplinary Learning

Although in the real world people use knowledge from various disciplines in an integrated form to solve problems and perform their jobs, the US education system typically breaks areas of knowledge apart into specialized studies, especially at the secondary school level where content becomes more demanding. When school subjects and courses are taught separately and disconnected from each other, students move from class to class and grade to grade, acquiring bits and pieces of knowledge. However, no one teaches students how these pieces relate to each other or how to synthesize knowledge from more than one subject. This fragmented approach is not an effective way to prepare students for life beyond school.

Education should increase students' understanding of the interconnectedness of knowledge. That's why the Rigor/Relevance Framework supports the belief that we learn best when we acquire knowledge in the context of a coherent whole and when students can connect what they are learning to the real world. The Rigor/Relevance Framework places the learning of skills such as reading, math, the scientific method, and writing in the context of a real-world topic that is both specific enough to be practical and broad enough to allow creative exploration.

Teachers may organize the standards requirements of their curriculum (both process skills and content knowledge) around a learning unit. In the study of a river basin, for instance, the curriculum might meet math standards by having students calculate water flow and volume; social studies may include the nature of river communities; science topics may involve phenomena such as weather and floods; and literature might include nonfiction and novels that are river focused, such as works by Mark Twain, as well as Toni Morrison's writing about *The Adventures of Huckleberry Finn.*

Curriculum and instructional tasks that integrate school subjects are a great way to add rigor and relevance, and typically cost little — no new textbooks, no additional equipment, and no bureaucratic reorganization or retraining of teachers. Often, all that is required of teachers is a change of attitude and the willingness to restructure instruction to not only meet standards but also to prepare students for life beyond high school and college. With some understanding of how skills are used outside school, an interdisciplinary curriculum increases the relevance quotient. Allocating instructional time can involve changes in the class schedule and new combinations of classroom hours, field trips, team teaching, and use of outside experts. Assessments may involve presentations to the school or community.

Beyond the Classroom Walls

One of the best strategies for bringing relevance to the classroom is to think beyond the walls of the school to community resources. Communities offer a wealth of opportunities for learning through application. Manufacturing plants, retail and wholesale businesses, hospitals and clinics, local government agencies, and nonprofit organizations are gold mines of technical reading materials, situations requiring good communication, scientific phenomena, and problems in search of solutions. You can arrange site visits or convene meetings of community leaders to brainstorm ideas. Some business leaders are willing to spend time in schools explaining to students the application of skills or posing real-world problems for them to solve. Elected officials, service organization leaders, recent graduates, and senior citizens can also help to identify learning opportunities in the community. Finally, schools can greatly enhance teaching and learning by creating partnerships with the community. Examples of partnership activities include mentorships, experiential learning opportunities, and co-investigations where students and community members solve problems together.

Planning for Interdisciplinary Learning

Below are the series of steps you will want to go through as you use the Rigor/Relevance Framework to plan for interdisciplinary learning. Ideally, you could also reach out to other teachers in your school to exchange content information and experiences.

1. **Determine the key points of intersection between disciplines that correspond to the standards outcome you want your students to reach.** As you investigate each cross-disciplinary idea in more depth, keep that standard outcome well in mind. It's easy to become enthralled by the idea itself and lose sight of the major instructional intent. Some ideas will probably need to be discarded, either because they are too complex or because they do not fully address the standards.

2. **Decide on the assessment.** Product or performance? Will students research, write, compute, model, demonstrate, build, survey, or report in a variety of academic, technical, work, and community environments? Review the instructional task and related assessment. Is this instructional task appropriate for your students? Will the assessment provide an accurate way to assess student learning? Make modifications as necessary.

3. **If planning for high levels of rigor as in Quads C and D, identify the prerequisite skills and knowledge that students must possess in each discipline.** Interdisciplinary instruction can fail if students lack knowledge of key concepts within each discipline.

4. **Consider if students must have additional information or skills before they can accomplish the rigor of the task you have assigned.** Sometimes you can teach needed skills or pieces of information rather quickly.

5. **Develop activities that cross the boundaries of disciplines in a purposeful way.** Conceptual mapping, in-class debates, group projects, and a variety of discovery techniques are examples of ways to accomplish this objective. Consider how students will use and incorporate technology.

6. **Identify organizations or individuals—in your community or online—who you or your students may want to reach out to.** The multidisciplinary instructional tasks almost always include real-world situations or problems.

Be intentional about the levels of rigor and relevance the students will practice. The richest interdisciplinary learning experiences draw on all four quadrants.

Technology for Rigor and Relevance

I have met many experienced educators who feel intimidated by students' proficiency with advanced technology. Indeed, today's students are digital natives and very comfortable with technology. They do not know of a world without the internet, computers, social media, and smartphones. In many cases, they began using technology at an incredibly early age, some as young as two years old, like my son Jeffrey. Their parents may have introduced technology as entertainment or learning aids. However, following the latest "cute couple" on YouTube or posting the "perfect" picture on your Instagram is not the same thing as using technology for authentic learning purposes. As educators, our job is to teach students how to use digital tools and media in ways that are similar to how they will be used in the workforce—to solve difficult problems, to communicate and share ideas at a high level, to create models, and to be persuasive. Using technology to support the Rigor/Relevance Framework will help support this goal.

Technology can produce a positive impact on achieving rigor and relevance by equalizing learning access, increasing learning effectiveness and efficiency, and creating new learning opportunities. For example, technology offers great potential to make the same information available to all students, regardless of their location or size of the school library. Teachers are now able to expand student learning beyond the classroom walls and to advocate for the technology infrastructure, materials, and activities that expose students to high-quality learning experiences.

Research shows that *how* technology is used is key. Simply using online learning to replace strong, positive student-teacher relationships is not beneficial. Esteemed educator Linda Darling-Hammond and her colleagues, however, found that technology can aid learning for high schoolers who are at the greatest risk of failing courses or dropping out when it's interactive, used to support discussions and projects with peers and teachers, and serves as a tool for creation rather than passive consumption.[3]

Blended Learning

Blended learning is not new. It's likely you and your students are already practicing some form of blended learning if they are using the internet to do any form of online learning. School districts have been moving in the direction of blended learning for some time; the school closures as a result of the 2020 Covid-19 pandemic have accelerated educators' acceptance of blended learning and brought along many who did not initially embrace it.

Blended learning is all about integrating technology into rigorous and relevant lessons. With blended learning, the student, rather than the teacher, is the person using and interacting with the technology. Students use the technology to help them solve a problem, research a topic, or communicate with others. Students are able to control the pacing and scheduling of their learning, or even the location from which they will complete online work.

It's easy to confuse blended learning with what's called a technology-rich classroom. In the latter, a teacher may present lessons using slides, host assignments and quizzes online for student access, and have students use Google Docs and online graphing calculators. These are all examples of using technology to enhance traditional instruction. But they do not fundamentally shift instruction to give students some element of control. Ideally, a blended learning approach ensures that students are engaged and are driving their individual learning experiences. With blended learning, students can rotate between self-paced, online learning and face-to-face instruction. This approach can help cater to individual student learning needs and offer flexible time frames that give students agency over the pace of their learning. Blended learning is important because it breaks down the traditional walls of teaching, ones that don't work for all students. To learn more about blended learning, take a look at Weston Kieschnick's *Bold School*, a book that clearly outlines blended learning that works. It is an incredible resource.

Technology and the Four Quadrants

Technology should be integrated and used to support engaging, standards-based instruction. Technology is not on one side and curriculum on the other. We use technology for students to do things they couldn't do without it, not as an add-on or what ICLE associate partner and author Eric Sheninger calls "a digital pacifier." For example, to enhance rigor, students can turn to the internet for a large number of online courses and enrichment activities. For relevance, there is no better way to apply communication or research skills than by interacting with experts, international students, and even government officials via the internet.

Technology also provides teachers with tools to enhance instruction by going beyond what is in a textbook. Figure 5.1 lists a few ways that students

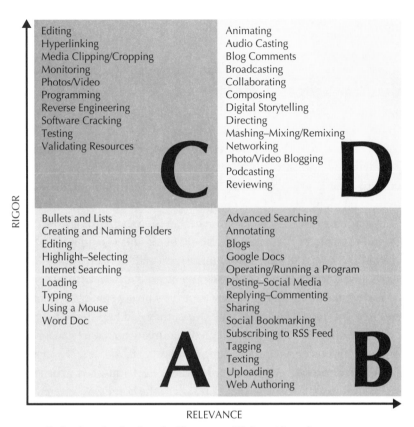

Figure 5.1 **Technology Applications for Rigorous and Relevant Learning**

can use technology for learning in each quadrant of the Rigor/Relevance Framework.

When deciding how to use technology in each of the four Rigor and Relevance quadrants, there are some general guidelines, as well as some overlap. For example, a Quad A task may be something as simple as learning how to use a Word document or searching online for a piece of information. Quad B tasks that use technology might be writing or providing commentary on a particular blog. In Quad C, students use higher level thinking skills to, for example, write computer code or search source material online to validate the accuracy of information. Quad D level activities might include digital storytelling or publishing a podcast.

Bump It Up

Remember Cliff from the opening of this chapter? When we first met, he wanted to better engage his students through learning experiences that involved high levels of rigor and relevance, but he wasn't sure his struggling students could handle more challenging material. We worked together to "bump up" his instructional planning.

Here's what we did: Cliff had an upcoming unit on electrical circuits. Typically, he would introduce the unit by asking students to define the important vocabulary (Quad A). Then, he would assign them reading from a science text along with related comprehension questions to answer (Quad A). Finally, he would show his students a video explaining how circuits work and then assess their understanding of circuits (Quad A).

With intentional planning, we bumped up Cliff's lessons so that his students could experience more rigor and relevance. To introduce the lesson, Cliff told his students to imagine that they were now newly employed technicians at the electric company. As these employees, they had to respond to a service call from a homeowner who complained that many appliances and switches throughout his home were not working. The students' job, as technicians, was to figure out the problem with the homeowner's electrical system, then recommend a solution to the issue so that all power in the home was restored (Quad D). Throughout this series of lessons, learning will take place across all of the four quadrants. And based on the structure of the task, we know that students will have to engage in Quad D learning to reach a final solution.

Teach Up! Instructional Planning Guide

The Instructional Planning Guide will help to focus and fine tune your purpose when planning assessments and instructional tasks by allowing you to become more intentional about how you assign levels of rigor and relevance. By stopping to consider each of the questions in the Planning Guide that concern outcomes and standards, assessment, and instructional tasks, you will have to think through the appropriateness of assigned tasks.

Notice that when considering outcomes, you can draw upon multiple standards, even if you make one standard the primary focus of instruction. This is when you will also want to be thinking about the interdisciplinary connections you can make to increase relevance. Whether you choose to have student assessment take the form of a product or performance, make sure that its level of rigor and relevance matches the levels of learning and instruction. If it's too easy, an assessment will not challenge students. If it's too difficult, an assessment may damage your students' confidence.

When designing instructional tasks, you want to be sure that you have correctly labeled the levels of rigor and relevance so that they land squarely in one of the four quadrants. If your instructional tasks only emphasize low levels of rigor, you are not giving students the opportunity to be exposed to the higher levels of rigor that are embedded in each of the standards. On the other hand, if your instructional tasks ignore the lower levels of rigor entirely, your students may not be prepared for Quad C and Quad D learning. Becoming purposeful in how you label levels of rigor and relevance ensures that student learning draws from each of the four quadrants. The following is my Instructional Planning Guide. You can also find a reproducible version in Appendix 6 or download it from www.Leadered.com/TeachUp.

Teacher Name:
Grade Level:
Content Area:

Outcome/Standards: Which standards will be the focus of instruction?

Primary standard(s):

Interdisciplinary connection(s):

Assessment: How will students show mastery of the standards?

Product/Performance:

Level of Rigor:

Level of Relevance:

Student Task(s): What will students do to gain proficiency with standards?

Task 1 Description:

Technology Integration:

Level of Rigor:

Level of Relevance:

Task 2 Description:

Technology Integration:

Level of Rigor:

Level of Relevance:

Task 3 Description:

Technology Integration:

Level of Rigor:

Level of Relevance:

The Instructional Planning Guide is meant to be used regularly and routinely. Although at first it may take some adjustments and tweaking, continued use should make it second nature!

Learning—and Loving—the Quads

As you become more comfortable and proficient in using the Rigor/Relevance Framework, you will get more of a feel for what each of the four quadrants offers and demands. Quads A and C are organized primarily around making sure that tasks progress in the level of rigor, from recalling facts and demonstrating understanding to problem solving and analysis. Quads B and D are organized primarily around how knowledge can be applied to real-world situations that are both predictable and unpredictable, with the goal being to increase relevance.

Through my work as a consultant, I have noticed teachers can struggle with designing lessons that fall into a specific quadrant. During my coaching sessions, I often find myself asking teachers the following question: "How can you enhance this task so that it solidly falls in your planned quadrant?" By grappling with this question, teachers can design more focused tasks that meet their expectations. This is particularly important when designing lessons or tasks intended for Quad D. To help, Chapter 6 will focus exclusively on what constitutes Quad D instruction. Quad D learning experiences can be among the most thought provoking, memorable, and exciting that you and your students will share. It also offers the type of learning that will best prepare them for their futures.

KEY TAKEAWAYS

- The Rigor/Relevance Framework follows the recent research and innovations in education that finds these three elements—curriculum, instruction, and assessment—are not separate and linear but are instead interrelated. In the new model, planning becomes a question of dynamically linking all three components.

- Instructional planning begins with the desired student outcomes and then works backward to figure out appropriate instructional tasks.

- Instruction and assessment planning often occur together, which means that it's important to choose an assessment type that matches the student work. Assessments generally fall into two categories: product or performance.

- Instructional planning should focus on what students will *do*. Using the four quadrants to gauge the level of rigor and relevance embedded in instructional tasks is a way to assure that you are on track to truly teach the standards. It can take a little practice to make sure your instructional tasks align correctly and that your intentions match up with your actions.

- Interdisciplinary learning that draws on standards from more than one subject increases students' understanding of the interconnectedness of knowledge, bumps up rigor and relevance, and is an efficient use of instructional time.

- Technology should be integrated into rigorous and relevant lessons, not used as an add-on. With blended learning, the student is using and interacting with technology to help solve a problem, research a topic, or communicate with others. They are also able to control the pacing and scheduling of their learning, increasing their sense of agency.

6

The Quad D Classroom Experience

Early in my career, I had the opportunity to work for Teach For America. I was brought on board to design a new teacher certification program that would secure state approval from the Georgia Professional Standards Commission. To design the program, my team first conducted extensive research on the existing state laws. We collaborated with regional and national staff to determine which components of Teach For America's current programming could be incorporated into the new program. We also worked with local universities and certification providers to investigate how their programming satisfied state requirements. Once the new certification program was designed, the budget was determined, and all artifacts were housed electronically, we presented our proposal to the state.

Although I didn't call it that at the time, my experiences with Teach For America exemplified the Quad D learning approach. *My team and I were tasked with solving a real-world unpredictable problem*: to design an alternative certification program and secure its approval by the state. *We had to think creatively* about how the program would meet the state requirements. *We drew upon skills learned in multiple discip*lines that included English language arts, math, and technology. *We collaborated with others*—internal staff, university partners, local education agencies—to exchange ideas and think outside the box to ensure that our design would meet the needs of our new teachers. *Finally, we presented our proposal to a real audience*, the Georgia Professional Standards Commission to be *assessed*. I'm proud to report that our program was approved with no conditions. Designing the certification program was tremendously engaging and meaningful for me professionally. I was motivated by its relevance and challenged by its rigor. Ultimately, it was a powerful learning experience.

Make It Authentic

The more their instruction mirrors authentic, real-world experiences, the more prepared your students will be for life and learning outside the classroom walls. Always look for ways to connect your students to the heart of the world. Engage with the surrounding community through its parks, local stores, and organizations. Arrange for your students to connect with a businessperson, a politician, or a community advocate. Bolster work with real-world tools and materials such as multimedia creation apps, tablets, and manipulatives.

As educators, our goal is to prepare students to be highly functioning members of society, whether we teach them how to read in the lower grades or how to construct logical arguments in high school. The ability to read critically and argue persuasively using logic is a life skill they will use no matter their future course in life! The ability to apply knowledge from a variety of sources to solve complex problems or to create real-world products are types of Quadrant D learning. One of the ways we can make sure we thoroughly prepare students for postgraduation challenges is to expose them to Quad D instruction that makes use of the Rigor/Relevance Framework. We want students to learn by engaging in tasks that are rigorous—addressing the high ends of Bloom's taxonomy—and relevant, giving them the opportunity to solve real-world problems.

In this chapter, you will learn more about how to implement Quad D tasks and learning experiences. First, I will show what it looks like for teachers to experience Quad D learning in an Idea Lab held at the Model Schools Conference, and then I will show how to bring Quad D experiences into the classroom. I will also discuss how to assess Quad D learning tasks and introduce you to some relatively easy strategies for creating Quad D moments in your classroom. First, though, let's talk about the role of student engagement in learning and how Quad D experiences can promote just that.

Student Engagement to Teach Up!

Student engagement is essential if all students are to achieve the skills and knowledge that will provide the basis for success and fulfillment throughout their lives. If students are engaged, they have the confidence and motivation to learn and are more likely to enroll in rigorous courses that apply higher-order thinking skills to real-world, unpredictable situations. They begin to make connections from one content area to the next as well as about themselves and their individual learning process. Teaching up is all about increasing student engagement.

Student engagement is the positive behavior that indicates full participation in the learning process. When students are engaged, we can hear, see, and feel their motivation in completing a task, taking pride in their work, or going beyond the minimum work required. Engaged students demonstrate a feeling of belonging by the way they act, the positive things they say about school, and their passionate involvement in class activities. True engagement is more than behaviors; it is about students being connected with their heads and their hearts.

You probably know that increasing student engagement is not easy. Student engagement is not about students complying with rules and the absence of poor behavior. Simply telling or encouraging students to engage themselves in their classwork is seldom enough, especially if learning is centered around repetitive and routine tasks. Quad D instruction that delivers high-rigor and high-relevance lessons helps students see where they can apply and use newly acquired skills and knowledge and leads to engagement.

The Idea Lab for Quad D Learning

To show teachers what engaged, Quad D learning looks and feels like, my colleague Dr. Erika Tate and I, along with some of the teachers we coached, designed a Quad D Idea Lab experience for the International Center for Leadership in Education's (ICLE) annual Model Schools Conference. The Idea Lab consisted of hands-on activities that leveraged digital technologies and physical materials for Quad D Learning. We set up four separate stations, and at each station participants were given access to a Google site that provided them with an authentic problem and instructions for working toward a solution. Participants could choose to engage in the tasks as a practitioner, who applies their knowledge of the tools or technologies to solve an authentic problem, or a producer, who has the opportunity to create a product or performance that leverages the tools or technologies. They also had to figure out how to work cooperatively with the other participants at their station without any facilitation. After about 20 minutes, we asked everyone to stop what they were doing, debrief for about five minutes, and then move on to the next station. To give you a sense of what it was like, I've included the instructional tasks for two popular Idea Lab experiences: "MonuMaker" and "Classroom Re:Design." As you read these tasks, think about how they embody Quad D learning.

MonuMaker

In this task, created by Miranda Evans, a high school social studies teacher, the Idea Lab participants were told that the Office of the City Planning in Orlando, Florida, working in conjunction with the National Park Service, was accepting bids to design a memorial for a new city park space. Two of Orlando's most powerful activists had donated acreage for the park with the stipulation that a memorial be designed and erected that focused on civil rights, war, or the military.

Participants who chose to be a practitioner were given makerspace supplies and tasked with recreating a model that was based on an existing memorial. First, they used the internet to find specific memorial images and read about important design aspects. Once they had absorbed the information, they were asked to *recreate a monument* using clay, cardboard, construction paper, straws, and other creative supplies. Participants who chose the role of producer were presented with the same scenario, but were asked to *design a new monument* that was inspired by the one provided. In both roles, participants had to write a description of the model that included a rationale for their design. Finally, they used a cellphone or tablet to upload the model's picture and description in what was essentially a bid to the park organizers.

Classroom Re:Design

In this task, I designed a Quad D Idea Lab experience where participants were invited to become involved in developing the campus for the soon to be opened School of the Future in Orlando, Florida, by sharing their vision for how to design classroom spaces. Each classroom was to embody a 21st-century learning environment that would enhance communication, collaboration, critical thinking, and creativity. The designers of the classroom that was the most innovative and best aligned with the criteria would work directly with an innovative leader of furniture for K–12 environments to design the classroom spaces in the new school.

Participants who chose to follow the practitioner pathway were tasked with researching what a 21st-century learning space might look like by finding at least three pictures online that contributed to communication, collaboration, critical thinking, and creativity and downloading those images to their device. Next, they used a collage-making app to design a collage with the images they'd collected. They posted the collage into a portfolio app and created an audio segment that justified how their images might encourage and support the classroom design objectives.

Producers were tasked with creating an actual model of their classroom designs using Play-Doh. They took photos of their model, uploaded it to the portfolio app, and created an audio segment that justified how their product could enhance communication, collaboration, critical thinking, and creativity.

The instructional strategies embedded in these tasks promoted choice, facilitated differentiated learning, and fostered academic discussion. Educators were encouraged to be creative in completing Quad D tasks and to reflect on how the tasks increased their own engagement. Giving teachers the opportunity to engage in the Quad D Idea Lab as students was a very powerful experience. When the teachers at the conference reflected on this task, they called the experience "transformational" and highlighted how it helped them understand Quad D instruction. Ultimately, the experience served as a model for teachers that they could use directly with their students.

Creating Quad D Tasks for Your Students

Educators often think that creating Quad D tasks will be more work. I used to feel that way myself. If I knew that my students needed to learn how to multiply, I would teach them the algorithm for multiplying three digits by two-digit numbers, and then give them the problem sets to practice that skill. After that I would move on to long division or whatever was the next standard they needed to know. But here's the problem. My students understood the process for multiplying three digits by two-digit numbers, but they had no idea when and how they would use that skill. The only reason for them to learn was to get the correct answer and do well on the test.

In a Quad D learning task, students still need to learn how to multiply, but they are also given the opportunity to actually use those skills to solve some type of authentic problem. They learn that skills are not compartmentalized but can be drawn on to solve all kinds of problems. Plus, in continuing to practice a particular skill they are gaining proficiency in ways that are more relevant than simply doing more worksheets with more multiplication sets.

Maybe you're thinking that you don't have time to do the deep work of a Quad D project. Keep in mind that one instructional task can bundle together a number of standards that students need to learn, thereby making your planning and classroom time more efficient. Instead of spending a few days on each individual skill, students will be able to master multiple standards within one task.

Another way that Quad D instruction is efficient has to do with your role during classroom time. When the learning experience begins, you're responsible for making sure all the materials are in order and that students understand their task. However, once students are engaged in Quad D tasks and working together, as they are for the majority of the time, you become more of a facilitator. Instead of standing up in front of the class for the entire block, you are freed up to move around the classroom and provide individual support to students. Groups of students may be stuck or struggling with different aspects of their task, and you can tailor your support to the needs of various groups.

Producer and Practitioner

Central to Quad D instruction, whether in the Idea Lab or in the classroom, are the two learning pathways called practitioner and producer. The practitioner pathway typically asks the participant to research, analyze, or report on existing information. The producer pathway usually asks the participant to go a little deeper into the instructional task and create something new. For example, a practitioner writes a report that analyzes an existing art exhibit whereas a producer analyzes the exhibit in order to produce something new that extends the thinking inherent in that particular exhibit.

Incorporating Student Choice

TEACH UP! TIP

Student choice is a critical part of Quad D learning experiences. Invite student choice with **the problem**, **the process**, and **the product** by deciding how much or how little structure you will provide within the task you assign students.

- Tell students the problem, but let them choose the process to solve it.
- Outline the process and the problem to solve, and let students choose the final product that will represent their thinking.

Drawn from Moving Beyond Quadrant A *by Bernadette Lambert.*[1]

Students can choose whether they want to learn as a practitioner or a producer. Neither role is better than the other. What's important is giving students a choice about which path they want to adopt as a way to exercise control over their learning process and how they will master a given set of standards. As one set of experts put it: "Students who associate a choice with feeling autonomous, competence, and in relationship with others are more likely to be engaged with the learning."[2]

As teacher-facilitator of a Quad D learning experience you want to let the students figure out as much as possible their individual roles and how they will work together. Collaboration, which requires students to form learning relationships, is another important aspect of the Quad D experience. Some students or groups might need more direction than others, and of course you will want to step in as necessary, but ideally you don't want to assign tasks or roles. One of the goals of the Quad D tasks is for students to figure out how to manage on their own and work productively together with their peers. This is an essential skill that will prove beneficial for students in college, the world of work, and beyond!

A Quad D Classroom Experience

Let's examine in detail how one middle school teacher created a dynamic, engaging Quad D experience for her students called Art + Science = Activism.

This days-long project, designed by educational consultant Dr. Erika Tate, contained two major learning objectives: (1) interpret the meaning or purpose of a piece of art and (2) design a prototype of a new media artwork that explained the causes or consequences of unclean water and encouraged environmental advocacy.

Students formed collaborative groups (named Artist Collectives) in which they took on roles based on expertise or passion. The roles were defined as below:

- **Art Director:** led the collective in identifying the vision for the artwork; ensured the artistic and technical details to achieve the vision.
- **Media Director:** guided the collective on the selection of physical and digital media; provided technical assistance in the use of media to convey meaning.
- **Communications Director:** composed the description of the artwork; ensured that the artwork and description encouraged advocacy and raised awareness.
- **Science Director:** advised the collective on the causes and consequences of unclean water; shared scientific resources that informed or inspired the artwork.

All directors were also contributing artists to the new media artwork.

Students were introduced to a public exhibition on clean water they could view online that had been produced by the Environmental Protection Agency (EPA) in partnership with *Smithsonian* magazine. Examples of the artwork included a water tower constructed of cardboard that would deteriorate over time, accompanied by music to sound like cardboard ("Water Proofing" by J. Pouwels and "Slough" by Joshua Marquez); a sculpture of a drinking fountain with yellow water arching from the spigot in front of a brick wall that bears a sign with the word "Colored" ("Flint" by Ti-Rock Moore); and a video composed of aerial footage shot by drones and a spoken word ode to Standing Rock Reservation in North Dakota ("We Are in Crisis" from Dylan McLaughlin and artists). Student practitioners were first tasked with selecting one of the artworks and interpreting its meaning. Next, they had to design an artwork similar in meaning to an existing piece in the collection. As a final step, they shared their artwork by posting it to a designated site. The posting included a title, the name of the artists, the media used, and an artists' statement.

Student producers also organized into collaborative groups with the distinct roles listed above and followed similar steps as the practitioners. However, they had to select two or more artworks from the EPA/Smithsonian collection and generate a theme for their mini-collection. They were also tasked with designing a new media artwork that extended or countered the themes of two or more of the existing artworks.

I hope you can see how Art + Science = Activism engaged students! At different times they were discussing, learning collaboratively, designing collaboratively, and teaching one another. In true Quad D fashion, the instructional tasks were interdisciplinary: ELA, art, and science. They demanded higher levels of rigor, including the option to disagree with the artwork themes. Addressing the very real environmental problem of clean water was a clear application of relevance. The tasks addressed multiple standards, including the ability to integrate and evaluate multiple sources of information in diverse formats and media in order to address a question or solve a problem. So much learning happening efficiently and simultaneously!

For more examples of Quad D learning experiences that involve students in collaborative work and integrate technology into the assessment, see the following boxed section. These experiences include making videos about a famous historical figure who persisted despite encountering some kind of failure (to learn about a growth mindset); building miniature furniture models out of centimeter cubes and then sketching the design on graph paper (to learn about dimensions, volume, and scale); and writing a magazine piece about the negative or positive impact of technology on social change that

QUAD D LEARNING EXPERIENCES

The Impact of Technology on Society

Created by Venola Mason

TIME for Kids magazine is looking for new original pieces to be published in their special winter edition. As an aspiring journalist, submit an editorial piece that examines the impact technology has had on social change.

http://bit.ly/ImpactTechnology

Storytime Is Ozo Fun

Created by Dr. Erika Tate

Ms. Book, a librarian at your local library, is looking to incorporate Ozobots into her upcoming story time block. Help Ms. Book by using your expertise with Ozobots to bring stories to life for her students.

http://bit.ly/StoryTimeOzo

Smithsonian Zoo: Habitat Design

Created by Kelly Gilstrap

The Smithsonian Zoo is looking to build a new habitat for an endangered species. As employees of Conservation Nation, students must create a research-based pitch to convince the zoo to choose their animal.

http://bit.ly/SmithsonianZoo

Science + Art = Activism

Created by Dr. Erika Tate

The Environmental Protection Agency (EPA) has partnered with the *Smithsonian* magazine to produce a public exhibition on clean water. Your class has been commissioned to create and curate a collection of new media artworks that encourage the public to advocate for clean water for all.

http://bit.ly/SciArtActivism

Flip Your Mindset

Created by Kristin Gainer

TED Talks is hosting an event in your area with the theme "Bigger Than Us" and is looking for new talent. As an up-and-coming new speaker, you will submit an audition video to be considered for this event.

http://bit.ly/FlipMindset

MonuMaker

Created by Miranda Evans

The Office of Planning in Cherokee County is working in conjunction with the National Park Service and accepting proposals to design a memorial for a new city space. Design a memorial focused on civil rights, war, or the military in order to be considered for funding by two powerful anonymous donors.
http://bit.ly/MonuMaker

Classroom Re:Design Challenge

Created by Venola Mason

The opening of the School of the Future in Orlando is this fall. As a founding member of the teaching staff, you have been invited to participate in the development of the campus. Create an innovative classroom design that embodies 21st-century learning principles to be considered for the actual classroom spaces.
http://bit.ly/ClassroomReDesign

Design for IKEA

Created by Kristin Gainer

IKEA is looking for a new design for a piece of furniture to be prominently showcased in their main showroom. Work as an independent designer or as part of a design team to create a piece of furniture to be considered for the display.
http://bit.ly/DesignIKEA

students could submit to a national competition. When planning Quad D learning experiences you will find that some will be brief one-off instructional tasks (see the Quad D Moments in Every Class section later in this chapter) and others will take place over a series of learning blocks, culminating in a finished performance or product that can be assessed.

Assess for Each Standard

Quad D tasks are among the most rigorous, relevant, and relational you will teach and that's in part because they are by definition interdisciplinary. This allows students to make real connections between different subjects. For this reason it's important that students be assessed for each of the standards that the Quad D task is designed to teach.

For example, if the task includes both ELA and science skills, you will have to design an assessment for the outcomes in each discipline. If students are writing a persuasive essay about the need for clean water, the assessment must include both the understanding of the science content (clean water) and how well they have mastered the elements of a persuasive essay. Assessing for only one standard means that students are unlikely to make connections that go beyond the superficial. They may focus only on the information about clean water or focus only on composing a written essay without having mastered both standards. Nor will they make the connection that persuasive writing is necessary to communicate the need for clean water.

When planning Quad D learning experiences, be very intentional about which content standards the instructional tasks will address. Using the Rigor/Relevance Framework can confirm that each task addresses rigorous content in an authentic way. Then make sure you have designed an assessment for each of those standards. Remember that student outcomes can take the form of product or performance. One of these outcomes can satisfy both standards (as in the example of the persuasion paper about clean water), but students must understand from the beginning of the assigned task that they will be assessed for both the rigor of the science and the rigor of the writing. If this seems like a daunting task, especially for secondary teachers, remember it's a great opportunity to connect with a colleague from a different discipline—chances are you'll gain a better understanding of how their content connects to yours and deepen a professional relationship.

Quad D Moments in Every Class

Quad D instruction does not have to be elaborate or require a lot of preparation. Nor does it require a lot of resources. Quad D can be quiet moments that you can drop into the day, use to open a lesson, or incorporate into existing instructional tasks. Below is a list of my top eight quiet moments, with a few examples for each strategy to give you an idea of their applications.[3]

1. **Around You.** This strategy asks students to think analytically and assists in building the relevance of a curriculum as it relates to themselves, their local community, work, or other real-world materials. Examples include collecting data about themselves and analyzing it mathematically, generating a family tree when studying genetics, or comparing an ad from a foreign country with one from their own.

2. **At Your Service.** This strategy links classroom learning to opportunities outside the classroom. Students identify or perform a simple act or service that would benefit individuals, the school, or the neighborhood. Service learning might include growing a garden and donating the vegetables to a food pantry, visiting a senior center, or participating in a neighborhood cleanup.

3. **Current Events.** Teachers can use this strategy to help students in any grade level or any subject connect content to real-world current events. Have students read and write blog posts or opinion pieces. Have students read three different media sources on one current event and then compare and contrast how it was reported. Stage mock debates about a controversial issue after students have researched different points of view.

4. **How Did That Happen?** Students use cause-and-effect analysis to determine why a real-life phenomenon, event, or action occurred. For a science class, students can explain the relationship of cause and effect to describe research related to natural disasters such as tsunamis, earthquakes, tornadoes, and hurricanes. Social-emotional learning can have students reflect on a behavioral problem to analyze how it happened and what the parties involved might have done differently to result in a better solution.

5. **Justify Your Position.** With this strategy, students take a position on a real-world issue that impacts someone and develop a rationale to defend it with a logical argument and citation of facts. For example, when studying the Bill of Rights, give students scenarios in which someone's rights may have been denied. Ask students to take a point of view concerning whether or not this was a denial of rights and to justify their position. Or have students bring in

articles about current environmental issues. Randomly assign students to take a point of view; then give them a few minutes to develop a rationale and state a position on this particular issue.

6. **Original Answers.** Central to learning with rigor and relevance, Original Answers emphasizes the process of learning rather than merely the acquisition of knowledge. Students arrive at a unique answer to an open-ended problem or create an original way to display knowledge or data. Have students brainstorm school rules they do not like or that they think need to be fixed. Ask groups of students to create a "better" rule and share it with the class. When reviewing math concepts, give students an answer and ask them to create different questions that yield the same answer. As students generate multiple questions, place these on the board and challenge students to come up with even more questions that yield the same answer.

7. **What If?** Students analyze a current condition and imagine the impact of change. This strategy can be used with historical events, in the middle of reading a story, or in a mathematical operation. Ask students to predict what the present might be like if a historical event turned out differently, how they think the story might end, or how an X-Y graph might change if a certain intervention occurred.

8. **"Why" Questions.** Students pose "why" questions on content for inquiry, exploring additional learning, or reflect on why learning is important to their lives or future. Have students write down what they want to learn about a particular topic. List questions they would like to ask the author of a book they've read. Pose why questions as writing prompts and then have students share their responses with the rest of the class.

By no means is this an exhaustive list. These Quad D moments are only the tip of the iceberg! Use them as inspiration to creatively modify and adapt to the subject and grade level you teach. The goal is to raise the level of rigor and relevance in your classroom in ways that increase student curiosity, engagement, and outcomes.

Learning and Loving Quad D

Quad D learning experiences are both a necessary extension and a natural enrichment to instruction. If you feel tethered to textbook instruction in order to make sure you will cover what your students need to know for your particular grade level, you might begin by mapping out how much time is allotted in a given semester for each standard. When I have coached teachers in this way, they usually find more time to spend on concepts than originally anticipated. As you become more comfortable and proficient in creating Quad D moments and learning experiences, you will get a feel for when to depart from textbook instruction and how to incorporate the rigor and relevance of Quad D. When student tasks are more rigorous, engaging, and interdisciplinary and allow them the opportunity to use what they have learned to problem solve and create solutions, you too will inevitably become more engaged.

Chapter 7 will show you how you can branch out beyond your individual classroom to make a school-wide impact with relationships, rigor, and relevance. School culture is key to these efforts. Becoming a teacher-leader by sharing your ideas and experiences with other teachers is empowering for them, their students, and for you!

KEY TAKEAWAYS

- If students are engaged, they have the confidence and motivation to learn. Quad D instruction helps students see where they can apply and use newly acquired skills and knowledge that lead to engagement.
- When educators complete Quad D tasks that promote choice, facilitate differentiated learning, and foster academic discussion, they find it a powerful experience that serves as a model they can use directly with their own students.
- Quad D instruction is an efficient use of teachers' planning efforts because it bundles together a number of standards into one task. When teachers are classroom facilitators for Quad D tasks, they are freed up to provide individual support to students.
- Students can choose the role of practitioner or producer during collaborative Quad D learning experiences. Giving students a

choice about their role is a way to exercise autonomous control over their learning process.

- The practitioner tasks usually ask students to research, analyze, or report on existing information. The producer tasks usually ask students to go a little deeper into the instructional task and create something new.
- Because Quad D learning experiences are interdisciplinary, it's essential that students be assessed for each of the standards that the task is designed to teach.
- Quad D instruction does not have to be elaborate or require a lot of preparation. Nor does it require a lot of resources. Quad D can be quiet moments that you can drop into the day, use to open a lesson, or incorporate into existing instructional tasks.

7

A Teach Up! Culture and Community

Not long ago I did an instructional walk through a high school in Missouri with a social studies teacher named Ryan. As I walked around the building and looked at bare walls, it was difficult to tell what was important to the school. There was very little posted, even in the front entranceway. What did they celebrate? What were their values? The physical building did not reflect a school culture or community.

Contrast this environment with Ryan's classroom. The walls were covered with completed student work, pictures that reflected various cultures and perspectives pertaining to study units, and posters with inspiring quotes from historical figures. We sat down to talk and when I complimented Ryan on what a great culture he seemed to be creating, he nodded and then looked thoughtful. He was trying to figure out how to help the school environment resemble the welcoming energy of his classroom, but he wasn't sure it was his place to tell others what to do. "I don't want to step on anyone's toes," he said.

We talked a little more, and I encouraged Ryan to meet with his principal or assistant principal and invite them to visit one of his class periods so they could see how his students interacted in that room and how much pride they took in interacting with such an intentional and stimulating physical space. The next time I talked to Ryan he told me that the administrators had visited and had been very excited by what they saw. They wanted to work with Ryan to figure out how to duplicate some of what he was doing so that it could be apparent outside of the classroom walls and in the school hallways. The principal was putting together a team of teachers to figure out how to redesign the front entrance of the school and the main hallway so that it was more welcoming and reflective of the school community.

Several months later when I visited the school I was uplifted by all the changes I saw, heard, and felt! The walls were freshly painted in appealing colors. The art teacher had hung student drawings and paintings and also exhibited some small clay figurines in a glass-covered case. Some of that art connected with the interdisciplinary learning units that classroom teachers had begun to initiate. Instead of the harsh bell that formerly rang between classes, the music teacher had arranged for soft music to play during those hectic transition times to encourage students to peacefully focus as they went from one class to the next.

By the way, having a school environment that is cheerful and welcoming, and well maintained, clean, and designed for traffic flow, feels pleasant and inviting to us because of how the environment affects the brain. Marian Diamond, the celebrated brain scientist from the University of California, was one of the first to clearly point out that an enriched environment effects dendrite formation and the thickening of the cortex, thereby enhancing brain growth and development.[1] In other words, when we enrich our student's environment, we are also enriching their brains.

Ryan felt pleased and empowered to have managed to spread some of the good cheer from his classroom to the rest of the building. In helping to change the culture of the school so that it became warmer and more welcoming, he was setting the stage for increased well-being and connection. He was also excited to have worked as a team with other teachers in the school. Rather than feeling he had "stepped on their toes," the other teachers felt inspired and were making plans for what they would do next to continue making an impact.

In this chapter, you will learn about how to make an impact beyond your classroom by becoming empowered as a teacher-leader who finds allies and establishes relationships with your colleagues. I'll remind you of the key roles that collaboration and communication among the adults in the building play in establishing school-wide rigor and relevance and share tips for involving students' parents. The second part of the chapter addresses the importance of community and how you can help create or maintain it in your school. But first, let's talk about the importance of culture, learning relationships, and the interplay between the two.

Culture as Curriculum

Culture is formed by our perceptions, values, and practices. As Terrence Deal and Kent Peterson eloquently write in their seminal work, *Shaping School Culture*:

> For decades terms such as *climate* and *ethos* have been used to try and capture this powerful, pervasive, and notoriously elusive force. We believe the term *culture* provides a more accurate and intuitively appealing way to help school leaders better understand their school's unwritten rules and traditions, customs, and expectations. The unofficial patterns seem to permeate everything: the way people act, how they dress, what they talk about or consider taboo, whether they seek out colleagues or isolate themselves, whether they work together, and how teachers feel about their work and their students.[2]

In other words, culture is the way things are. Culture is an organization's personality. Culture is the way the hallways look and whether people greet each other in those hallways and how students feel about coming to school each day when they walk down the hallways.

The culture of a school is imperative to its success; arguably even more important than the academic curriculum because when students have a positive feeling toward their school, they tend to achieve better. The authors of *How to Create a Culture of Achievement in Your School and Classroom*, Douglas Fisher, Nancy Frey, and Ian Pumpian, believe that the culture of a school is so important that it should actually be considered as a second, implicit curriculum.[3] Although implicit, this culture shouldn't be a secret, rather it should be part of an ongoing dialogue between teachers, students, administration, and parents. Culture doesn't just happen. Culture is not static. It's the accumulation of the thousands of interactions, practices, and artifacts that take place in individual classrooms and throughout the building. Culture is dynamic, but to change and maintain a culture takes careful planning and daily practice.

A School-Wide Culture of Positive Relationships

In a Teach Up! culture that values strong relationships to support student learning that is rigorous and relevant, positive relationships must also exist among the adults in the building. Those adults include teachers and administrators, as well as classified staff—lunchroom monitors, bus drivers, librarians, specialists, and so on. When learning relationships are the concern of every adult in the building, everyone understands why relationships are so critical and their role in reinforcing them. Students are more likely to make a commitment to relationships and to engage in rigorous learning when they know that the adults in their world care about how well they do.

Teachers in the building must also connect with one another to form positive relationships. When teachers support and celebrate one another in ways that build camaraderie, it not only feels good, but also helps everyone to work together more efficiently and effectively to implement rigorous and relevant learning. And all of that positive energy translates down to the students. They pick up on the feeling between the adults in the building! The better the relationships that teachers have with one another, the more you will want to collaborate, and the easier it will be to naturally collaborate and share ideas. All the best practices around rigor and relevance will be more likely to be implemented school-wide. What's more, when adults are collaborating, that behavior serves as a model for how the students can relate to one another and work together.

You're Never Just a Teacher

In my years as an educator, I have heard so many teachers say, "I am just a teacher." Usually that phrase is an expression of their feelings of powerlessness or an explanation of why they must put up with unsatisfactory conditions of one kind or another.

You're never "just" a teacher. As your practice evolves you should feel empowered to share practices and take steps to effect the change you want to see. The anthropologist Margaret Mead famously said, "Never underestimate the power of a small group of committed people to change the world. In fact, it's the only thing that ever has." Similarly, a small group of teacher-leaders can not only make a difference in the lives of their students but also change the culture of a school. You don't have to have the title of an administrator to make an impact beyond your classroom; you have a lot more influence on your school and community than you think. When you see yourselves as part of a system and can find people who can support you and people you can reach out to ask for help in that system, then you're becoming a teacher-leader.

Once your instructional planning hits all the four quadrants and your students are learning along the higher levels of rigor and relevance, you can be a model for others. Think about what you can share with others in your school and who are most ready to be allies. Can you make a presentation at a teachers' meeting? Volunteer to do professional development for other teachers in your building? Maybe you can even take on a more formal leadership role such as grade level or department chair. You don't have to wait for the principal or another administrator to call a meeting!

Certainly, you can start a private social media group where you and your colleagues can share ideas and ask for help. You can begin a group with only a few other people who are in your building, grade level, or content area. As you share strategies and instructional tasks, you're likely to interest other teachers. Over and over I have seen how positively teachers respond to the leadership of fellow teachers. Reaching out to others and forming alliances with one another is how your role begins to change from "just" a teacher to teacher-leader.

Collaboration Is Key

Studies have shown that while most teachers work alone, they desire more collaboration with their colleagues. Research has also shown that schools are more effective when teachers have opportunities to observe and help one another, and participate in any ongoing cultural or instructional changes.[4] Teachers are more likely to make changes in their teaching if they see their

TEACH UP! TIP

Ideas for Strong Teacher Collaboration

- *Share it!* Share work products digitally—somewhere that's visible and easily accessible.
- *Schedule it!* Schedule time for collaboration.
- *Team up!* Create intentional, thoughtful collaboration teams.
- *Tool up!* Consider agendas and processes to keep the collaboration productive.

Adapted from Keeping the Door Open to Collaboration *by Emelina Minero, Edutopia*[5] coworkers attempting similar changes and have opportunities to discuss ideas, challenges, and implementation. Students are not the only ones who learn better when they enjoy learning relationships that support academic rigor and relevance—teachers learn better too!

To implement school-wide strategies for creating a positive, welcoming, and inclusive environment for all students requires teachers to communicate on an ongoing basis and genuinely collaborate. School staff need to work together to create a school climate that's warm, welcoming, and inclusive. School culture cannot thrive when each individual class does its own thing as disjointed parts. Interdisciplinary activities among classes for Quad D projects as well as simple knowledge of what is going on from one class to the next help to bring everything together.

One of the most influential things you can do is to invite people into your class so that they can see the level of instruction and how engaged your students are in their learning. Too often principals and other administrators come into teachers' classrooms only if something is wrong. But if principals can see for themselves, they will understand the impact of what you're doing and often they will want to know more. As happened with Ryan, whom you met at the beginning of this chapter, they may ask you to share your practices in a faculty meeting or professional learning community.

Teachers, I've found, don't have the opportunity to go into one another's classrooms often enough, but it's an easy way of encouraging informal collaboration and exchange strategies. Visiting a colleague's classroom during instruction is of course not an occasion to judge or evaluate, but a way of becoming exposed to others' practices and ideas. Dropping in at the end of the day, when the students are gone, can also be a good time for the informal chat that lends support or imparts information.

Teacher-to-Teacher Observation and Review

Peer observation is the official term for teachers observing other teachers, and the practice is universally endorsed by education groups. No matter how informal or formal, the objective is always the same — help teachers improve instruction and implement school-wide best practices. If a review will be involved, have a clearly defined process that outlines the roles and responsibilities of the reviewers and the teacher whose work is being reviewed. Equally important is a set of criteria for the review. This guides the teacher's work and provides the reviewer with a focus for commenting on that work.

Visiting one another's classrooms in a formal manner is an opportunity for staff to reflect on strengths and weaknesses and to work together to improve and implement best practices. The overall goal is to establish a culture of relationships that stimulates rigor and relevance. Through the observation process, teachers can periodically examine and reflect on where they stand in relation to their goals for teaching and learning. To make teacher-to-teacher observations truly valuable, it's best they take place over three consecutive sessions:

1. Discussion about teaching prior to delivery of instruction
2. Classroom observation
3. Discussion about teaching after delivery of instruction

Having another teacher in the classroom for a review can initially feel threatening. That's why it's important to have established a rapport of trust and mutual respect and a well-defined focus around a specific lesson or teaching method.

Sharing Student Work

A big part of teaching is looking at students' work. Teachers assess, grade, and comment on classwork and homework. They may also use samples of student work as models for diagnostic purposes. However, teachers typically look at their students' work on their own rather than with colleagues. A powerful way to establish a culture of learning relationships is to organize groups of teachers to look at student work. If students in your class are doing a performance-based assessment, that's the perfect time to invite other teachers—and possibly the students in other classrooms—to be part of the audience. You can also share links to online sites where student work may be found.

Collaborative Teacher Groups and Professional Learning Communities

Some of the most valuable learning comes from regular conversations among small groups of teachers that focus on a single topic. Instructional planning using the Rigor/Relevance Framework lends itself especially well to small-group collaborations. You may want to discuss how to plan assessments that measure specific standards. Collaborative teacher groups are the perfect venue for meeting up with colleagues and coordinating interdisciplinary Quad D learning experiences.

Remember that if people are too busy to meet in person, videoconferencing and other digital aids make for flexible scheduling and locations. One of the best professional experiences I have had was the three years that I co-hosted the #AchieveItChat on Twitter with one of the teachers I coached, Kristin Gainer. The digital forum gave me the opportunity to connect with educators across the country around very specific topics, such as building relationships with students, integrating technology into instruction, and self-care for educators. We shared ideas, resources, and practices that could be used immediately in a classroom or school setting, and I formed some lifelong professional relationships that I value deeply.

Involve the Parents

Years ago, when I was a teacher at an inner city school I learned how powerful it can be to engage the parents of the children in my classroom.

At the beginning of the school year, when teachers handed out a list of requested supplies, one of my colleagues easily counted parents out. "You know, these parents, they're not going to be engaged," she said. "Don't expect much," advised this veteran teacher.

A week passed. The parents of my students were coming into my room nearly every day with boxes of supplies. Pencils, markers, tissues—everything on my list! Soon the tables in the back of the room were piled high. My coworker who told me not to expect much stopped by. "Ms. Mason,

TEACH UP! TIP

Parents Are Key

Remember to focus on parents! Don't delay on building strong relationships with parents; connect early in the school year. The aim is to gradually establish trust via many positive interactions with parents. Once established, this trust foundation will go a long way if any issues arise that may lead to difficult conversations.

how did you get your parents to bring in all that stuff? I got only a box of pencils from one parent."

I told her it was because of the relationships I'd established with the parents. Since the first day of school, I'd reached out to all of them. When they dropped off their kids in the morning, I made sure I was at the door to say good morning. At the end of the school day, I went outside during pickup so I could talk to the parents and engage them with things I'd noticed about their child. "Oh gosh, Jimmy seems like he's such a great reader," I told a parent whose son had read a chapter book that week. "Sylvie is so good with math already," I told a parent whose daughter had been absorbed in geometric figures. "She's a shining star." The parents saw that I cared. They began to see me as a person who was part of their child's team, more like a family member rather than someone just doing a job. So when I asked for supplies and I kept my expectations high, the parents came through. Every parent wants to know that their child's teacher cares. Every parent wants to hear positive feedback about their child. Over time, more and more parents became engaged with the school.

Welcoming Parents

Contributing classroom supplies is one of many ways that parents can connect to a school in meaningful ways that support learning and relationships. Sometimes it is the parent or a group of parents who steps in and makes all the difference to help everyone in the school take a break and come together. Here are a few ways that you can encourage or invite parents to become involved.

- Help decorate school hallways for a holiday or special event.
- Plant or care for a school garden.
- Classroom visits. Many parents have interesting skills, jobs, or interests to share. Do you have a parent with a military background or who plays in a band?
- Staffing after-school events. Parents can help serve pizza, sell books at book fairs, or even organize materials for small groups.

You can welcome parents near the beginning of the school year by sending out a letter that lists specific ways they might help. Update the letter as the year continues by letting parents know about individual learning units that you are planning. The better you know the individual parents of the children in your room, the more you will be able to draw on their specific interests or skills. What's more, forming good relationships with parents can help you better understand and connect with your students.

Creating a School-Wide Community

If all staff work to build meaningful relationships with students, which includes wrapping their arms of support around students who may experience difficulty and holding students to high academic expectations by exposing them to rigorous and relevant instruction, students will thrive in the type of environment I describe in this book.

Important to mention is that well-designed forms of communication are critical when creating a school culture where people can connect and collaborate. This includes everything from the school's website, emails, phone calls, newsletters, media blurbs, etc. Keeping parents and the community informed of all of the positive things happening at school builds goodwill that supports you as teachers and the academic success of your students.

School Events

School-wide events both promote and reflect the culture and community of the school. The atmosphere and connectedness of these events help students feel as though they belong. Although the activities themselves do not have an academic focus, the relationships that develop as a result of these experiences prime students for academics and to be successful academically. In other words, if students are excited about events at school and feel like they belong, they will be more likely to come to school and participate enthusiastically in learning that has rigor and relevance.

Students can contribute ideas for school events. Doing so gives them ownership and makes them more likely to buy into the activities. Remember that the connected feelings and relationships that make up community can come from smaller groups and activities as well as large-scale events. After-school clubs and activities also help students strengthen relationships to their peers, the school, and their individual learning goals. Keep in mind that parents and local community members may be able to support and donate time and resources to your school—often people do want to help and be involved, they just don't know how.

The simplest way to create community is to be intentionally present and caring not only in your classroom with your students but also in the hallways, at school events, and with your colleagues. In addition, there are plenty of vibrant and fun ways to create community with school celebrations—that when repeated year after year become rituals or traditions—and recognitions of individual accomplishments. Some of the suggestions in the list below may be familiar and others may be ones you will want to try!

- Develop a social media presence to share accomplishments, activities, and updates with teachers, students, parents, and the community at large.
- Celebrate students and teachers and their achievements with awards and recognition.
- Feature classroom stories on the school website.
- Plan and host themed lunches.
- Make time to collaborate during professional development days.
- Celebrate and share student triumphs in classrooms.
- Post student achievements, such as college acceptances and projects, in the hallways and on bulletin boards.
- Give "gotcha" awards—teachers or administrators give these to students when they catch them being a positive school community member.
- Interact and play with students during recess.
- Play upbeat or peaceful music over the intercom system before and after school and during transitions when students are moving in the hallways.
- Carve out time on Monday morning to let students talk about their weekend.
- Hand out vouchers for free entry to school sports, plays, or other activities as rewards and incentives.

A lot of these ideas are simple and often quick and easy to plan, but they are invaluable in bringing everybody together and priming students for academic achievement. And again, making these things happen comes back to the positive relationships that enable collaboration and communication. As teacher-leaders, you set the tone for the school and the building. Creating a community culture takes just that, a community of teachers, administrators, students, and parents.

Be a Teach Up! Team

When I first moved to Atlanta, I saw a notice that a local nonprofit, Coan Park Tennis Association, was offering free tennis lessons. I signed up because I thought it would be a fun way to get exercise and meet people. And that has turned out to be true. Monday mornings, when I came to my classroom, I loved when my students asked if I'd won any games that weekend. But here's the truth: I continue to play tennis not because I like winning or because of the exercise I'm getting, but because I'm having fun with the friends I've made. We joke around and hang out after the matches. We have so much fun together that we quickly forget how hot or cold it is outside or how strenuous some of the matches can be. We push one another to do our best and to perform at our highest levels. When we win, it just makes the experience that much better. We're all on the same team.

Promoting a Teach Up! culture means that you become part of a team in your school. Once you have established relationships, rigor, and relevance, your influence can extend beyond your individual classroom and throughout the whole school. You have a larger circle of influence, a larger team of positive educators, now. You can make a difference in the lives of more students, helping to ensure a better future for *all* of them. You can take pride and satisfaction in seeing your students reach their full potential. Teach Up!

KEY TAKEAWAYS

- Culture is formed by our perceptions, values, and practices. The culture of a school is imperative to its success.
- In a Teach Up! culture that values strong relationships to support student learning that is rigorous and relevant, positive relationships must also exist among the adults in the building.
- You're never "just" a teacher. As your practice evolves, you should feel empowered to share best practices and contribute to the school culture.
- While most teachers work alone, they desire more collaboration with their colleagues. Schools are more effective when teachers have opportunities to observe and help one another and participate in any ongoing cultural or instructional changes. To

implement school-wide strategies requires teacher to communicate on an ongoing basis and genuinely collaborate.

- One of the most influential things you can do is to invite people into your class so that they can see the level of instruction and how engaged your students are in their learning.
- Reaching out to the parents of your students to let them know you care means you can all be on the same team supporting the learning that goes on in your classroom.
- School events create relationships and community as a way to prime students for academic success.
- Promoting a Teach Up! culture means that you become part of a team in your school that brings out your best teaching and makes a difference in the lives of that many more students.

Appendixes

1. Relationships Framework (Chapter 1)
2. Relationships Rubric (Chapter 2)
3. Nine Relationship-Building Strategies (Chapter 2)
4. PAUSE and REACT Tool (Chapter 3)
5. Rigor/Relevance Framework (Chapter 4)
6. Instructional Planning Guide (Chapter 5)

For downloadable versions of the appendixes, please go to
www.Leadered.com/TeachUp

Appendix 1

Relationships Framework

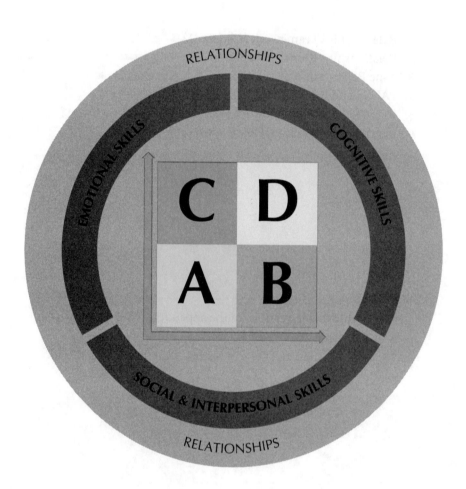

Appendix 2

Relationships Rubric

Connection	Beginning	Emerging	Developed	Well Developed
Student Learning	• Student learning artifacts and how students talk about their work show no evidence that they understand how their interests, passions, culture, and/or personal/family lives can be relevant to learning and foster connection with teachers and classmates. • Students are not given opportunities to and/or do not share details of their personal interests and lives.	• Students occasionally incorporate their interests, passions, culture, and/or personal/family lives into their learning. • Some students can identify some of their strengths and talents and/or indicate feeling safe asking for help when learning stretches beyond current strengths.	• Students can identify some strengths and talents and are encouraged to apply them in their learning, particularly when it aligns with their interests, passions, culture and/or personal/family lives. • When prompted, students demonstrate feeling safe asking for help or sharing struggle, personal or academic, with their teacher.	• Students feel safe volunteering their interests, passions, culture, and/or details of their personal/family life with peers for the sake of sharing with, learning from, and connecting with each other. • Students show their trust for their teacher by initiating questions, asking for clarity when they need it, and vocalizing personal or academic struggles.
Instructional Design	• Learning tasks do not yet regularly involve student interests, passions, culture and/or personal/family lives. • Teacher and student interactions are centered primarily on academic content; there is little evidence of interactions based on students' interests, passions, culture, and/or personal family lives.	• The teacher devotes some time to getting to know each student on a personal level to foster trust; begins to discern students' strengths and weaknesses; and learns about students' interests, passions, culture and/or personal/family lives. • Some time is devoted to delivering personalized, scaffolded instruction to connect individually with students and meet their current learning needs.	• Teacher habitually asks students what interests them and helps them incorporate this into their learning in a way that leverages their strengths. • Teacher intentionally plans multiple opportunities within a lesson to ask students if they need help or support and scaffolds and/or personalizes instruction as needed.	• Lesson plans, learning tasks, and tools empower students to self-direct learning based on their interests, passions, culture, and/or personal/family life and encourage family involvement whenever possible. • Instruction is scaffolded and personalized whenever possible to meet each student where he or she is.

Compassion	Beginning	Emerging	Developed	Well Developed
Student Learning	• Student behavioral issues and high stress/tension are common in the classroom. • Disproportionalities are evident in classroom participation, disciplinary issues, and some or most students appear to hold biases towards each other.	• Student behavioral issues (and their punitive responses) and interruptions can sometimes derail learning. • Productive and positive engagement is evident in more than one student demographic group.	• Students demonstrate support and/or sympathy for peers, particularly in moments of stress or misbehavior, and attempt to de-escalate stress and tension as it arises. • Students demonstrate a lack of exclusionary behavior, judgmental attitudes, or stereotype-based thinking towards peers and are open to learning from and with every classmate.	• Students have a set of productive stress reduction and coping mechanisms they apply on their own as needed, both for themselves and as suggestions to classmates. • Students self-regulate behaviors and contribute to a cohesive, positive, and compassionate classroom where every student has the opportunity to be seen, heard, and understood.
Instructional Design	• The teacher opts to punish a misbehaving student (punitive approach) rather than trying to understand and address the root cause with compassion (empathetic approach). • Teacher biases are evident in instructional delivery, expectations of students, learning structures, and/or interactions with students.	• The teacher occasionally uses flexible SEL instructional strategies to cope with and mitigate social-emotional, stress-related, or behavioral issues in real time. • The teacher makes an effort to engage students from all backgrounds and identities in classroom discussion and learning tasks.	• Teacher applies strategies to prevent behavioral issues from derailing instruction and holds private, appropriate conversations with disruptive students to understand and address the root cause and uses punitive measures infrequently. • Lessons are designed to cultivate empathy, foster understanding, and teach the value of compassion in the classroom.	• Teacher has cultivated a compassionate learning environment such that students self-mediate disruptions before teacher gets involved. • Teacher embodies and models empathy, and seizes opportunities for growing compassion for classmates and the culture at large.

Vulnerability	Beginning	Emerging	Developed	Well Developed
Student Learning	• In learning tasks or discussions, students do not use the language of growth and learning to address the typical emotional highs and lows of learning. • Unproductive feedback discourages students in the face of mistakes or perceived failures rather than offering constructive strategies to improve and grow.	• Students are exposed to the language of growth and learning through discussion and/or feedback and indicate some use of it on their own. • Students begin to reframe perceived failures or setbacks as an opportunity for growth and learning.	• Students understand the language of growth and learning and verbalize how it influences their self-perceptions as learners and motivates them to meet high expectations. • Students feel safe and validated expressing or honoring their feelings about learning, particularly their frustrations and the joys of overcoming challenges.	• Students voluntarily express how they felt as they struggled, made mistakes, and turned setbacks into learning opportunities; students can identify and explain their emotions. • Students demonstrate a positive self-perception as learners with unlimited potential and believe their teachers perceive them similarly.
Instructional Design	• Lesson plans include questions that ask students only what they learned, not also how they felt as they learned, precluding opportunities for teachers to validate and normalize students' emotional experiences. • Teacher uses fixed-mindset language (e.g., "You're smart," or "This is hard for you") and/or promotes low student learning expectations.	• Using the language of growth and learning in feedback or conversation, the teacher shares personal stories of learning struggles and how she turned setbacks into growth. • At least some learning tasks incorporate students' emotions and leave space and time for students to overcome challenges and practice bouncing back.	• Lesson plans include flexible and tailored SEL strategies to incorporate the language of learning and growth into conversation; the teacher is careful to acknowledge and validate students' emotional experiences as they are shared. • Teacher integrates multiple and varied opportunities for students to reflect on their learning and progress towards meeting high expectations, e.g., through journaling, self-assessment, goal setting, etc.	• Teacher allows students' natural emotions to emerge and is prepared with a broad knowledge of flexible SEL strategies to address and validate them in real time, such that social and emotional learning skills are seamlessly integrated into all learning. • Teacher makes a point to celebrate when students overcome challenges, meet high expectations, take risks, and discover new potential, demonstrating her belief in their potential as whole people.

The Relationships Rubric: An Overview and Guide

In building the Relationships Rubric, we are making an important leading-edge effort to create a framework for planning and observing positive relationships in the classroom, which create the necessary conditions for social and emotional learning. The effort is leading edge because research around teacher-student relationships is limited and can be challenging due to the often intangible nature of relationships. To build the rubrics, we reviewed available research and also relied on what we know to be true about human connection and helping students feel seen, understood, valued, and cared for. Ultimately, we distilled the core components of building and nurturing relationships in the classroom down to: connection, compassion, and vulnerability.

Connection

The goal of connecting with students is to establish trust. Without trust, we cannot have relationships. Research shows that trust is a byproduct of teachers connecting with students not just on an academic level but also on a personal level (e.g., learning students' interests, developing cultural competence and understanding students' cultures and home lives, engaging with students' families, etc.). This kind of connection, in addition to observing student work, also sheds light on students' strengths and weaknesses.

In the classroom, connection means:

- The teacher makes a regular and concerted effort to get to know students on a personal level.
- Students see their interests, passions, culture, and/or personal/family lives as relevant to learning and are given opportunities to incorporate them into learning tasks.
- As a result of knowing students' weaknesses, the teacher offers scaffolded and/or personalized support to meet students where they are and address weaknesses.
- Students know their strengths, learn how to leverage them in learning, and feel supported in addressing weaknesses.
- The teacher makes students feel safe asking for help, and students feel comfortable and no shame asking for help.

Compassion

When we extend compassion to others, we reject knee-jerk judgments, we mitigate bias, and we choose to lead with empathy. When teachers are compassionate, they view students as the whole children they are and make students feel seen, heard, understood, and cared for.

In order for a teacher to be compassionate, she must be self-aware; she must know her biases and take steps to eliminate them. She must also lead with empathy; this is particularly true in the face of behavioral issues, where compassion will help the teacher understand the root cause. When students receive compassion, they begin to feel capable of rising above any biased perceptions of them or self-limiting beliefs or behavioral patterns. Compassion is also the inroad to reducing behavioral problems, reducing disproportionalities, and establishing equity in instruction and learning. This is, in part, because brain research shows that *all* learning is social and emotional learning. Instruction that works to reduce negative perception of an individual student or certain demographic student groups, which can in turn contribute to those students' negative self-perception, promotes learning that nurtures social and emotional development and compassion for others.

In the classroom, compassion means:

- Instead of reflexively taking punitive measures when a student misbehaves, the teacher tries to understand the root cause of the behavior. The goal is to avoid labeling the student negatively and help the student create a new, positive behavioral pattern.
- The teacher has a range of flexible SEL instructional strategies to help defuse tension and behavioral problems and/or help students reduce stress in real time.
- Students have strategies to self-regulate behavior and help themselves and peers reduce stress.
- Students demonstrate compassion for their classmates.

Vulnerability

Vulnerability is perhaps the most opaque indicator and perhaps the most important. Brené Brown, a leading researcher on vulnerability, is leading a shift in how we perceive vulnerability. Where vulnerability has been known as a negative state, her research is showing that "it is the most accurate way to measure courage" and is a positive conduit to openness and growth. Brown defines vulnerability as "uncertainty, risk, and emotional exposure." Vulnerability asks us to experience and face with courage all of the emotions that come with risk-taking—from the positive ones when we succeed to the negative ones when we don't. On the other side of this is growth, resilience, and unconditional self-worth. Importantly, in facing and processing emotions, we move through them and can prevent them from festering and escalating to a point of self-harm (emotional or otherwise) or harm to others (emotional or otherwise).

The healthiest relationships are those where both parties feel safe being vulnerable. The goal of helping students become comfortable with vulnerability is two-fold: (1) to help them develop a positive self-perception as learners through an openness to healthy risk-taking and the capacity to persevere amid any outcome; and (2) to help them redefine having and facing emotions as a courageous act of strength, *not weakness*.

In the classroom, vulnerability means:

- Teaching students that learning is courageously vulnerable and presents typical highs (joy, satisfaction, curiosity, etc.) and lows (frustration, confusion, productive struggle, etc.).
- Using the language of learning (e.g. growth mindset language), engaging students in a dialogue about their emotional experiences as they learn, grow, confront and overcome setbacks, etc. so that emotions are normalized and validated.
- Reframing perceived setbacks and failures as normal, informative, and opportunities to grow and develop resilience.
- The teacher shows vulnerability by sharing personal stories of setbacks and growth.

Appendix 3

Nine Relationship-Building Strategies

Title	Description
Connection	
Joy Board	**Protocol** • Have students reflect on something that has made them happy (in the last week or month). • The students should find an image or draw a picture to illustrate their reflection. • Post the pictures on the Joy Board. This could be a physical board in your classroom or an electronic board. • Allow students to share and incorporate these things into the day as applicable. **Rationale and Connections** • Helps teacher and students get to know one another. • Allows students to reflect on the positive things that happen in their lives. • Helps students to see things they have in common. • Teachers can incorporate these things into the class to improve and maintain culture.
Classroom Meeting	**Protocol** Create an agenda with the following or similar components: • Greeting and announcements. • Review important culture pieces (being respectful, setting and meeting goals, maintaining a clean environment, paying attention, reinforcing rules or commitments). • Engage in a cooperative exercise or game. • Teacher and/or student shares something that is top of mind for them and others respond with questions. **Rationale and Connections** • This is a time to check in on the culture of the classroom and address any behavior or habits that negatively impact the culture. • It promotes cooperation and teamwork in a low stakes environment, which helps students work better together in small groups. • This helps students to feel comfortable sharing their culture/experiences and creates a safe environment.

Title	Description
In the Know	Protocol • Look for opportunities throughout the day to share information about yourself with students (culture, family, education, pets, music, hobbies, interests, weddings, births, deaths, etc.). Ask students questions about themselves and their lives. • Make connections between your life experiences and the content you are teaching. Ask students how their life experiences connect to content. • Make connections between your strengths and talents and your successes. Help students to identify and use their strengths and talents to help them learn. Rationale and Connections • The more you and your students know about each other, your relationships will be more authentic and the stronger your classroom culture will be. • As you all get to know one another they will feel more comfortable asking for help or sharing when they are struggling personally or academically.
Compassion	
Yes, That's Me!	Protocol • Identify a student to honor. (Make sure to mix up the order based on students who may be popular/unpopular, showing success/struggling, etc.) • Make sure to celebrate every student in the course of the semester/year. • Have all other classmates write an appreciation for this student on separate sheets of paper. • Read the notes aloud and allow the student who was honored to share how it felt being in the spotlight. Rationale and Connections • Students practice looking for the good in their classmates even if they have not developed a friendship, increasing the level of inclusivity. • Students who may not get many opportunities to be celebrated get their opportunity to be recognized in a positive way. • Student behavior improves because students are motivated to get caught doing good.
Notice! Empathize! Act!	Protocol • Teacher notices something going on between students. • She presents the situation to the class. • The class analyzes the situation, looks at things from different perspectives, and brainstorms how they should respond. • Eventually students begin to notice situations and present them to the class for consideration.

Title	Description
Notice! Empathize! Act!	Rationale and Connections • Students learn to become aware of how their actions impact others. • Students have the opportunity to see things from a different point of view and reflect on their feelings. • Students use feelings of empathy to drive different behavior.
Restorative Circles	Protocol • When a student gets in trouble, instead of automatically punishing them, allow them to fill out some premade cards that have starters on them "I _____. I did this because _____. I now feel _____." • Also allow other students and the teacher to share how this made them feel and how it impacted them. • As a class, come to consensus on a resolution. Rationale and Connections • Students become more self-aware when they can accurately reflect on their behavior and practice more self-control when they better understand their feelings. • Allows class to come together and decide on a course of action for why they want to do something. • Students have the opportunity to express themselves and show respect for each other's opinions.
Vulnerability	
Check the Tank	Protocol • Students quickly share their current mood using any of the following: emoji, song, #hashtag, etc. • Two or three students are invited to share their response along with an explanation to the class. • Students who are listening can ask a question, share a connection, or offer some advice. • The teacher listens and follows up with students who are in need. Rationale and Connections • This strategy gives students the opportunity to acknowledge and share their emotions. • Through this practice students will get comfortable working through negative emotions in a productive way and will also have the opportunity to share good news. • Students who are listening have the opportunity to empathize, connect, and offer up a positive resolution. • The teacher can check in with students, even if they didn't share an extended response, to see how they are handling their emotions and if they need a listening ear.

Title	Description
Level Up	Protocol • A student presents a situation to the class where they wish they had acted differently or there had been a different outcome. • The class listens, then students can volunteer to respond with how they would have handled the situation. • The student shares how (s)he handled the situation and how (s)he would do things differently if (s)he had the advice of their classmates during that time. Rationale and Connections • This strategy allows students to see that they have control over how they respond in various situations. • It gives them the opportunity to be reflective of their actions and think through how they can overcome mistakes and make better decisions.
Stretch Out	Protocol • Students think about what they would like to accomplish personally and academically during the school year. (Push them to set goals that seem difficult for them or that allow them to venture into something new.) • Students record no more than four goals in a journal (two personal, two academic). • In the journal, students create a plan for how they will meet their goals and document process and setbacks along the way. • Teacher reads the student journals periodically and shares insights with the students about their entries. • Students can also conference together in small groups to share setbacks and progress to get input from their peers. • As goals are achieved, students can share with the class what their goal was and how they went about achieving that goal including the setbacks and how they overcame them. Rationale and Connections • This strategy allows students to set ambitious goals for themselves and take the necessary actions to meet those goals. • The journal gives them the opportunity to document their experiences and track their progress. It can serve as motivation for the student to see how they are working around setbacks to be successful. • The peer conferences allow students to encourage and motivate one another as well share ideas. • The feedback from the teacher helps keep students on track toward meeting their goals and strengthens the connection between the teacher and the student. • It trains the students to be open about the challenges that are involved in learning something new or tackling something that is difficult.

Appendix 4

PAUSE and REACT Tool

 Pay Attention

Look for changes in disposition, behavior, or habits.

Ask Questions

Uncover the specifics behind why this change is occurring.
(I noticed...and I'm wondering...?)

Use Your Expertise

Determine if other adults should be involved.
(school psychologist, principal, parent, etc.)

Show Genuine Interest

Show the student that their well-being is important to you.

Evaluate the Circumstances

Review all of the evidence to determine a plan of action.

Reach Out

Create a team of support for the student.
(teachers, coaches, counselors, etc.)

Extend a Helping Hand

Provide direct support to the student.

Assume the Best

Presume postitive intentions.

Create Opportunities

Connect the student to opportunities within and outside of the classroom.

Tap into Their Greatness

Set the student up for success by building on their interests and strengths.

Appendix 5

Rigor/Relevance Framework

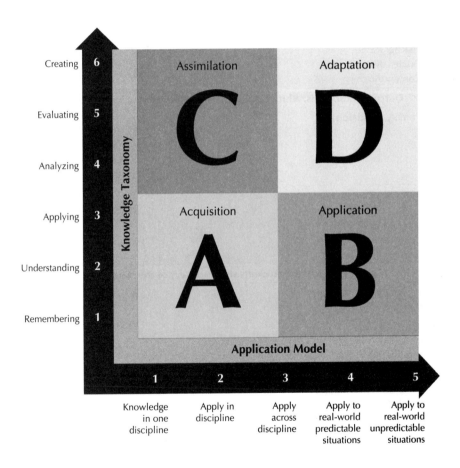

Appendix 6

Instructional Planning Guide

Teacher Name:
Grade Level:
Content Area:

Outcome/Standards: Which standards will be the focus of instruction?

Primary standard(s):

Interdisciplinary connection(s):

Assessment: How will students show mastery of the standards?

Product/Performance:

Level of Rigor:

Level of Relevance:

Student Task(s): What will students do to gain proficiency with standards?

Task 1 Description:

Technology Integration:

Level of Rigor:

Level of Relevance:

Task 2 Description:

Technology Integration:

Level of Rigor:

Level of Relevance:

Task 3 Description:

Technology Integration:

Level of Rigor:

Level of Relevance:

Notes

Introduction

1. Sanders, W. L., & Rivers, J. C. (1996). *Cumulative and residual effects of teachers on future student academic achievement* (Research Progress Report). Knoxville, TN: University of Tennessee Value-Added Research and Assessment Center; Wright, S. P., Horn, S. P., & Sanders, W. L. (1997). Teacher and classroom context effects on student achievement: Implications for teacher evaluation. *Journal of Personnel Evaluation in Education, 11*, 63.
2. Wright, Horn, & Sanders, 63.
3. Collins, J. (2001). *Good to great: Why some companies make the leap . . . and others don't.* New York, NY: HarperCollins.

Chapter 1: A Positive and Welcoming Culture for Learning

1. Daggett, W., & Jones, S. (2019). *Addressing whole child growth through strong relationships: The evidence-based connections between academic and social-emotional learning.* Boston, MA: Houghton Mifflin Harcourt; Cornelius-White, J. (2007). Learner-centered teacher-student relationships are effective: A meta-analysis. *Review of Educational Research, 77*(1), 113–143; Sherwood, C. (2019). Building positive student relationships. *SecEd, 2019*(9), 13–13.
2. Raanaas, R. K., Patil, G. G., & Hartig, T. (2012). Health benefits of a view of nature through the window: A quasi-experimental study of patients in a residential rehabilitation center. *Clinical Rehabilitation, 26*(1), 21–32; Drahota, A., Ward, D., Mackenzie, H., Stores, R., Higgins, B., Gal, D., & Dean, T. P. (2012). Sensory environment on health-related outcomes of hospital patients. *Cochrane Database of Systematic Reviews 2012*(3); Ulrich, R. S. (1984). View through a window may influence recovery from surgery. *Science, 224*(4647), 420–421; Ulrich, R. S. (1991). Effects of interior design on wellness: Theory and recent scientific research. *Journal of Health Care Interior Design, 3*(1), 97–109; Ulrich, R. S. (2002, April). Health benefits of gardens in hospitals (Paper for conference). International Exhibition Floriade, *Plants for People, 17*(5), 2010.
3. Rodrigues, P. F., & Pandeirada, J. N. (2018). When visual stimulation of the surrounding environment affects children's cognitive performance. *Journal of Experimental Child Psychology, 176*, 140–149; Rodrigues, P. F., &

Pandeirada, J. N. (2019). The influence of a visually-rich surrounding environment in visuospatial cognitive performance: A study with adolescents. *Journal of Cognition and Development, 20*(3), 399–410; Lopez, R. T. (2020). *Creating meaningful classroom environments: How do teachers' pedagogical beliefs affect the implementation of their visual displays in elementary classrooms?* (Doctoral dissertation, University of California, Los Angeles).

4. DeSilver, D. (2014). School days: How the US compares with other countries. Pew Research Center. Retrieved from https://www.pewresearch.org/fact-tank/2014/09/02/school-days-how-the-u-s-compares-with-other-countries/.

Chapter 2: Relationships: Strategies for Creating Connections

1. Brown, Brené. (2012) *Daring greatly: How the courage to be vulnerable transforms the way we live, love, parent, and lead.* New York, NY: Avery, p. 2.
2. Dweck, Carol. *(2006) Mindset: The new psychology of success.* New York, NY: Random House. p. 7.

Chapter 3: PAUSE and REACT: A Tool for Helping *All* Students

1. Centers for Disease Control and Prevention (CDC). (2019). Adverse childhood experiences. Retrieved from www.cdc.gov/violenceprevention/childabuseandneglect/acestudy/index.html.
2. Anda, R. F., Butchart, A., Felitti, V. J., & Brown, D. W. (2010). Building a framework for global surveillance of the public health implications of adverse childhood experiences. *American Journal of Preventive Medicine, 39*(1), 9; World Health Organization. (2009). Addressing adverse childhood experiences to improve public health. Geneva: WHO; Felitti, V. J. (2009). Adverse childhood experiences and adult health. *Academic Pediatrics, 9*(3), 131–132; Sacks, V., & Murphey, D. (February 20, 2018). The prevalence of adverse childhood experiences, nationally, by state, and by race or ethnicity. Child Trends. Retrieved from https://www.childtrends.org/publications/prevalence-adverse-childhood-experiences-nationally-state-race-ethnicity.
3. HRSA Maternal and Child Health. (2020). NSCH Data Brief 2020. Retrieved from https://mchb.hrsa.gov/sites/default/files/mchb/Data/NSCH/nsch-ace-databrief.pdf.
4. Hughes, K., Bellis, M. A., Hardcastle, K. A., Sethi, D., Butchart, A., Mikton, C., . . . & Dunne, M. P. (2017). The effect of multiple adverse childhood experiences on health: A systematic review and meta-analysis. *The Lancet Public Health, 2*(8), e356–e366.
5. HRSA Maternal and Child Health, NSCH Data Brief 2020.
6. Maguire-Jack, K., Lanier, P., & Lombardi, B. (2020). Investigating racial differences in clusters of adverse childhood experiences. *American Journal of Orthopsychiatry, 90*(1), 106; Zetino, Y. L., Galicia, B. E., & Venta, A.

(2020). Adverse childhood experiences, resilience, and emotional problems in Latinx immigrant youth. *Psychiatry Research, 293,* 113450.

7. Kwate, N.O.A., & Goodman, M. S. (2015). Cross-sectional and longitudinal effects of racism on mental health among residents of Black neighborhoods in New York City. *American Journal of Public Health, 105*(4), 711–718; Williams, D. R., & Williams-Morris, R. (2000). Racism and mental health: The African American experience. *Ethnicity & Health, 5*(3-4), 243–268; Williams, D. R. (1999). Race, socioeconomic status, and health: The added effects of racism and discrimination. *Annals of the New York Academy of Sciences, 896,* 173–188; Utsey, S. O. (1998). Assessing the stressful effects of racism: A review of instrumentation. *Journal of Black Psychology, 24*(3), 269–288.

8. Dorado, J., & Zakrzewski, V. (October 23, 2013). How to help a traumatized child in the classroom. *Greater Good Magazine.* Retrieved from https://greatergood.berkeley.edu/article/item/the_silent_epidemic_in_our_classrooms.

9. Myers, S. S., & Pianta, R. C. (2008). Developmental commentary: Individual and contextual influences on student–teacher relationships and children's early problem behaviors. *Journal of Clinical Child and Adolescent Psychology, 37*(3), 600–608; Campbell-Sills, L., Cohan, S. L., & Stein, M. B. (2006). Relationship of resilience to personality, coping, and psychiatric symptoms in young adults. *Behaviour Research and Therapy, 44*(4), 585–599; Skaalvik, E. M., & Skaalvik, S. (2007). Dimensions of teacher self-efficacy and relations with strain factors, perceived collective teacher efficacy, and teacher burnout. *Journal of Educational Psychology, 99*(3), 611.

Chapter 4: The Four Quadrants of Learning

1. Hamilton, T. (2019). LinkedIn hiring survey: Hiring for soft skills is key. *5 Rs Newsletter.* Retrieved from https://www.selectionresources.com/why-selection-resources/news/2019/04/10/2019-linkedin-hiring-survey-hiring-for-soft-skills-is-key.

2. Petrone, P. (2019, January 1). The skills companies need most in 2019—and how to learn them. *Learning Blog,* LinkedIn. Retrieved from https://learning.linkedin.com/blog/top-skills/the-skills-companies-need-most-in-2019--and-how-to-learn-them.

3. Bughin, J., Hazan, E., Lund, S., Dahlström, P., Wiesinger, A., & Subramaniam, A. (2018, May 23). Skill shift: Automation and the future of the workforce. McKinsey Global Institute. Retrieved from https://www.mckinsey.com/featured-insights/future-of-work/skill-shift-automation-and-the-future-of-the-workforce.

4. Cunningham, B. C., Hoyer, K. M., & Sparks, D. (2015). Gender differences in science, technology, engineering, and mathematics (STEM) interest,

credits earned, and NAEP performance in the 12th grade. *Stats in Brief.* NCES 2015-075. National Center for Education Statistics.

Chapter 5: Instruction for Today's Classrooms

1. Wiggins, G. P., Wiggins, G., & McTighe, J. (2005). *Understanding by design.* Alexandria, VA: ASCD.
2. Ainsworth, L., & Donovan, K. (2019). *Rigorous curriculum design: How to create curricular units of study that align standards, instruction, and assessment.* Rexford, NY: International Center for Leadership in Education, p. xix.
3. Darling-Hammond, L., Zielezinski, M. B., & Goldman, S. (2014). *Using technology to support at-risk students' learning.* Washington, DC: Alliance for Excellent Education.

Chapter 6: The Quad D Classroom Experience

1. Lambert, B. (2016) *Moving beyond quadrant A: Delivering rigor, relevance, and learner engagement in your classroom.* Rexford, NY: International Center for Leadership in Education.
2. Parker, F., Novak, J, & Bartell, T. (2017). To engage students, give them meaningful choices in the classroom. *Phi Delta Kappan 99*(2), 37–41.
3. International Center for Leadership in Education. (2012). *Effective instructional strategies—Quadrant D moments.* Rexford, NY: International Center for Leadership in Education.

Chapter 7: A Teach Up! Culture and Community

1. Diamond, M. C., Krech, D., & Rosenzweig, M. R. (1964). The effects of an enriched environment on the histology of the rat cerebral cortex. *Journal of Comparative Neurology, 123*(1), 111–119.
2. Deal, T. E., & Peterson, K. D. (2016) *Shaping school culture,* 3rd ed. San Francisco, CA: Jossey-Bass.
3. Fisher, D., Frey, N., & Pumpian, I. (2012). *How to create a culture of achievement in your school and classroom.* Alexandria, VA: ASCD.
4. Viadero, D. (2018). Teacher recruitment and retention: It's complicated. *Education Week, 37*(18), 4–5; Haun, D. D., & Martin, B. N. (2004). Attrition of beginning teachers and the factors of collaboration and school setting. *RMLE Online, 27*(2), 1–7; Shortland, S. (2010). Feedback within peer observation: Continuing professional development and unexpected consequences. *Innovations in Education and Teaching International, 47*(3), 295–304.
5. Minero, E. (August 24, 2015) Keeping the door open to collaboration. *Edutopia.* Retrieved from https://www.edutopia.org/practice/teacher-collaboration-matching-complementary-strengths.

Reflections